Richard Edward Dennett

Notes on the Folklore of the Fjort

(French Congo)

Richard Edward Dennett

Notes on the Folklore of the Fjort
(French Congo)

ISBN/EAN: 9783337232511

Printed in Europe, USA, Canada, Australia, Japan

Cover: Foto ©Suzi / pixelio.de

More available books at **www.hansebooks.com**

FJORT MOTHER AND CHILD.

Frontispiece.

NOTES ON
THE FOLKLORE OF THE FJORT

(FRENCH CONGO).

BY

R. E. DENNETT,

AUTHOR OF "SEVEN YEARS AMONG THE FJORT."

WITH AN INTRODUCTION BY

MARY H. KINGSLEY.

ILLUSTRATED.

LONDON :
PUBLISHED FOR THE FOLK-LORE SOCIETY
BY DAVID NUTT, 270-271, STRAND.

1898.

PRINTED BY
J. B. NICHOLS AND SONS,
PARLIAMENT MANSIONS,
VICTORIA STREET, WESTMINSTER, S.W.

PREFACE.

THE following collections reached my hands in a more or less fragmentary state. The bulk of the work had been written at one time, and little was needed to put it into a state for publication. But other portions, and those not the least important, had been written at different times and with different objects, and the task of weaving them all together in the author's absence was not a light one. Thus, though the author has read the proofs of all but Appendix II., it will be easily understood that the difficulties involved in passing a book of this kind through the press, while he was residing several thousand miles away, are such as to account for many imperfections, which would have been rectified had he been able himself to determine its final form and to superintend its publication. The sins of omission, of occasional repetition, and perhaps of occasional obscurity, that may be found, must therefore be laid at the editor's, and not at the author's door. I can only hope that the circumstances may be taken into account to extenuate these offences.

The difficulties I have referred to would, indeed, have been insuperable had it not been for the incessant help of Miss Kingsley. The debt due to her is by no means confined to the writing of her interesting and valuable introduction and the arrangement of Appendix I. She read all the manuscripts and selected in the first instance those most suitable for publication. Innumerable questions of detail have arisen in the course of printing, making it necessary to refer constantly to her, and in every case her knowledge of the country and the people, her time and thought, have been ungrudgingly placed at the service of the Folk-Lore Society. Lastly, she selected the photographs to be reproduced for the plates, and laid her own stock of negatives under contribution for the purpose of adding to them. It has been a matter of regret that the Society has been unable to avail itself to a greater extent of her kindness in this direction.

I am also indebted to Mr. W. H. D. Rouse for help kindly rendered in revising the Latin translation of the songs.

The orthography of the word *Fjort* has been adopted with some hesitation. Mr. Dennett has himself not always adhered to this form. In the chapter on the Death and Burial of the Fjort (which was communicated independently to the Society and published in *Folk-Lore*, vol. viii., p. 133), as it originally stood, he wrote *Fiote*. The pronunciation of the word would, I am informed, be more closely represented in ordinary English spelling as *Fceaught*.

E. SIDNEY HARTLAND.

Highgarth, Gloucester,
   July, 1898.

CONTENTS.

	PAGE
INTRODUCTION, BY MISS KINGSLEY ...	i.
I. THE FOLKLORE OF THE FJORT	1
II. HOW A NATIVE STORY IS TOLD	25
III. HOW THE WIVES RESTORED THEIR HUSBAND TO LIFE	33
IV. HOW NSASSI (GAZELLE) GOT MARRIED ...	35
V. THE VANISHING WIFE	39
VI. ANOTHER VANISHING WIFE	42
VII. THE JEALOUS WIFE	46
VIII. NGAMBA'S BALLOON	49
IX. THE WICKED HUSBAND	54
X. THE WONDERFUL CHILD	56
XI. HOW KENGI LOST HER CHILD	58
XII. THE TWIN BROTHERS	60
XIII. THE YOUNGER BROTHER WHO KNEW MORE THAN THE ELDER	65
XIV. THE CHIMPANZEE AND GORILLA	69
XV. THE ANTELOPE AND THE LEOPARD	71
XVI. HOW THE SPIDER WON AND LOST NZAMBI'S DAUGHTER	74
XVII. THE TURTLE AND THE MAN	
XVIII. KILLING A LEOPARD	80
XIX. THE GAZELLE AND THE LEOPARD	82
XX. THE WILD CAT AND THE GAZELLE	85
XXI. THE CRAFTY WOMAN OVERREACHES HERSELF ...	86
XXII. HOW THE FETISH SUNGA PUNISHED MY GREAT-UNCLE'S TWIN BROTHER, BASA	88
XXIII. THE RABBIT AND THE ANTELOPE	90

a *

CONTENTS.

		PAGE
XXIV.	THE FIGHT BETWEEN THE TWO FETISHES, LIFUMA AND CHIMPUKELA	94
XXV.	THE FETISH OF CHILUNGA	96
XXVI.	THE LEOPARD AND THE CROCODILE	98
XXVII.	WHY SOME MEN ARE WHITE AND OTHERS BLACK	101
XXVIII.	THE BIRD-MESSENGERS	103
XXIX.	NZAMBI MPUNGU'S AMBASSADOR	105
XXX.	WHY THE CROCODILE DOES NOT EAT THE HEN ...	106
XXXI.	THE THREE BROTHERS	108
XXXII.	DEATH AND BURIAL OF THE FJORT	111
	APPENDIX I.	117
	APPENDIX II.	150
	INDEX	164

LIST OF PLATES.

I.	FJORT MOTHER AND CHILD	*Frontispiece*	
II.	A BAKUTU WHO CAME TO LOANGO TO SEE NZAMBI	*To face page*	18
III.	FUNERAL SHIMBEC	„	113
IV.	PRINCE XIKAIA BY THE FUNERAL CAR OF HIS BROTHER, LINGUISTER FRANCISCO ...	„	114
V.	CLIMBING A PALM-TREE FOR PALM-WINE ...	„	121

NOTES ON THE FOLKLORE OF THE FJORT.

INTRODUCTION.

Ever since the Folk-Lore Society did me the honour to
ask me to write an introduction to these stories, I have
had a gradually intensifying sense of my incapacity to do it
properly. It is true that I am personally acquainted with the
tribe of Africans to whom these stories belong—that I have
heard many of them told in the way Mr. Dennett so accurately
describes—that I know Mr. Dennett personally, and am therefore
acquainted with the many claims that anything he may have to
say has upon students of primitive culture, because he speaks
on the subject of the Fjorts from a knowledge gained during
seventeen years of close association and sympathy with them,
and possesses also a thorough knowledge of their language.
Yet, these things notwithstanding, I still feel that someone
else should write this Introduction, because I am myself only
a collector of West African ideas, and these stories clearly
require a preface from the pen of a comparative ethnologist who
could tell you how the Undine-like story of the vanishing wife

got into Fjort folklore.   I can only say I have not only heard
this story, but I have known in the flesh several ladies whose
husbands were always most anxious that they should not hear
or see some one particular thing that would cause them to disappear, for ladies who have this weakness are always very
valuable.

And again, I cannot tell you how the Fjorts came by the
set of stories they and their neighbouring tribes possess regarding the descent into hell of living men, of which Mr. Dennett
gives the finest example I know of in the story of "The
Twin Brothers": nor yet again how they came by the Pro-
metheus-like story of "How the Spider won and lost Nzambi's
Daughter." All these explanations I must leave to the comparative ethnologist; but in so doing it may be as well to mention
a few things regarding the difficulties that present themselves,
even to the mere collector, in forming opinions regarding West
African folklore.

First, there is the difficulty of getting reliable information
regarding the opinion of the natives on things, as that opinion
at present stands.   Secondly, there is the difficulty of forming
an opinion as to why it stands in that form; whether it arises
from the native's uninterrupted observations of Nature, modified
by his peculiar form of intellect; or whether it is a white idea
primarily, but in a state modified by having passed through a
generation or so of African minds.

Regarding the difficulty of getting reliable information upon
native customs it is not necessary for me to speak at great
length, because it is now fully recognised by scientific students
of the subject.   The best way of surmounting the difficulty is
for the ethnologist to go and study the mind of the native

personally; but this method is not one easily followed in West Africa on account of the deadliness of the climate and other drawbacks. But even if this method is followed, as it was by Bastian, Buchholz, and Hubbe Schlieden, it is still greatly to the student's advantage to compare his own collected information with that of men who have been for years resident in West Africa, who are well acquainted with the native language, and who have had opportunities of observing the native conduct under all sorts of difficulties, dangers, joys, and sorrows—who have, as the old saying puts it, summered and wintered them. Unfortunately such white men are rare in West Africa; but so great is the value of their opinions in my eyes that I have always endeavoured to get the few there are of them to publish their information for the benefit of students of ethnology at home, instead of leaving these worthy people to the mercy of travellers' tales. Do not however imagine that I regard the traveller as, next to the mining expert, the most unreliable source of information extant. Even the African traveller has given reliable information on many things, but the conditions under which African travel is carried on are not favourable to the quiet, patient sympathetic study of the native mind; for that we must look to the white resident in Africa, the missionary, and the trader.

To give you an instance of the ease with which native customs might be badly observed by a traveller, I will cite an experience of my own when I (in spite of not being a true traveller but a wandering student of early law), nearly fell into error. Passing down a branch of the Karkola River in the Oroungou country, in a canoe with a choice band of natives for crew, we suddenly came upon a gentleman on the bank who equally suddenly gave several dismal howls and fired at us with the scatter gun prevalent in West Africa. Having a rooted antipathy to being fired at, and knowing that the best way to prevent a recurrence of the unpleasantness when dealing with a solitary native is to tackle him before he reloads, I jumped on to the bank. The man turned and fled, and I after him down a narrow bush-path followed at a discreet distance by a devoted member of the crew yelling for me to come back. I succeeded in getting hold of my flying friend by his powder-bag and asked him why he had behaved so extremely badly. Then, when the rest of the crew saw that the incident promised entertainment without danger, they joined us, and we found the poor man was merely suffering under domestic affliction. One of his wives had run away with a gentleman from a neighbouring village, and so he had been driven to fire at and attempt to kill a member of any canoe-crew from yet another village that might pass his way; because, according to the custom of the country, the men of this village would thereby have to join him in attacking the village of the man who had stolen his wife. So you see, if I had not minded being fired at, but just put down in my note-book that the people of this region were hostile savages and passed on, I should not have come across this interesting piece of native law, nor any of the other interesting pieces of native law I gained knowledge of during the subsequent palavers. This is only one instance of many which I have come across, wherein it would be almost impossible for a person rapidly passing through a country to form a true opinion regarding a native custom, and these instances have all confirmed me in my respect for the resident white man's opinion.

The missionary opinion has of late years been regarded by the ethnologist somewhat suspiciously, as being a biassed one, but, however this may be, we are very heavily indebted to the missionaries for the work they have done in native languages. This department is one to which the missionary has naturally devoted himself, because his aim in dealing with natives is to make them comprehend his teaching. He is, for many reasons, not so much interested in other parts of native culture. Their manners, customs, laws, and religions are, from his point of view, bad and foolish; but experience has taught him that the natives will listen to his teaching as soon as they can understand him, and therefore he is mostly content to leave alone the study of other things than the language, as little better than waste of time. There have been, however, several notable exceptions to this general rule. The works published by the Rev. J. L. Wilson,* the Rev. H. Goldie,† and the Rev. H. M. Waddell are of immense value, both from the great opportunities of observation these gentlemen had, and from their speaking of native customs and ideas with a knowledge of the native language. Unfortunately, the missionary who could surpass all these, valuable as they are, the Rev. Dr. Nassau, shows no sign of breaking the silence which afflicts all men who really know West Africa.

I cannot help thinking that the time has now come when it is the duty of some ethnologist to turn philologist for himself, with the assistance already provided for him by the missionaries, and work at African languages, not from the point of view of their structure, classification, and diffusion, but from that of their inner meaning, and I can safely promise him the discovery of an

---

* *Western Africa.* J. Leighton Wilson. London, 1856.
† *Calabar and its Mission.* Hugh Goldie. Edinburgh, 1890.

extremely interesting mass of matter. I feel sure that we cannot thoroughly understand the inner working of the African mind until this department of the study of it has been efficiently worked up; for the languages contain, and are founded on, a very peculiar basis of figurative thought, and until that is thoroughly understood we really cannot judge the true meaning of native statements on what is called totemism, and sundry other subjects.

The other resident white who lives in close contact with the native is the trader. I regret to say I can cite to you no book of reference on native customs by a trader in modern times, save Mr. J. Whitford's; * but in former days we had several, chief among which are those of Bosman,† Sieur Brue,‡ and Barbot; and the great exactness of these makes one all the more regret the absence of the West Coast trader from modern literature. I have done my utmost to induce many of the gentlemen whom I have had the honour to know personally to break through their silence and give us works again like Bosman's *Guinea*, they being by experience and knowledge so pre-eminently fitted to speak regarding native customs; and I think with regret of the perfectly irreplaceable library of knowledge that has been lost by the death of Captain Boler of Bonny, and Major Parminter, and of the other great collections of facts that Mr. Wallace, Mr. Bruce Walker, Mr. Hart, Mr. Pinnock, Mr. Forshaw, and several others could give us. Mr. Dennett is so far, however, the only one inclined to do anything else but shake his head in horror over the mis-statements circulated about Africans.

* *Trading Life in Western and Central Africa.* J. Whitford.
† Bosman's *Description of Guinea.* London, 1705.
‡ Labat's *Afrique Occidentale*, 1728.

The position of the trader towards the native is such as to make his information and observations particularly valuable to the ethnologist. The trader is not intent on altering the native culture to a European one; but he is intent on understanding the thing as it stands, so that he may keep at peace with the natives himself and induce them to keep peace with each other, for on peace depends the prosperity of West African regions in the main. We have not any tribe on the West Coast that subsists by war; we have no slave-raiding tribes that are directly in touch with the coast-trader;* but we have a series of middlemen-tribes through whose hands the trade from the interior passes to the latter. The middlemen system is in its highest state of development from the Niger to the Benito. Above this part—namely, in the regions of the Bight of Benin—the power of the middleman has been broken considerably by Mohammedan influence; while below, from the Benito to the Congo, it is now being considerably upset by the invasion of the Bafan from the interior, and the enterprise of the French explorers. To the south of the Congo it has long ago been broken by the Portuguese. Therefore the trader's greatest danger is now in the Niger districts, when a chief, on account of some quarrel, stopping trade passing through his district, may become a serious nuisance to the white man. The management of the chief, however, has in those regions now passed into the hands of the English government in the Niger Coast Protectorate, and into the hands of the Royal Niger Company in the regions of the middle Niger; so it is not so interesting to study the relationships of the native and the trader in those regions as it is to study those existing between the

---

* This statement does not include the Royal Niger Company, who have pushed up through the middle-man zone.

individual white traders, such as Mr. Dennett, and the native, as you can still find them in Congo Français, and in KaCongo and Angola. Here the trader is practically dealing single-handed with the native authorities, and is regarded by them in much the same light as they regard one of their great spirits, as an undoubtedly superior, different sort of creation from themselves, yet as one who is likewise interested in mundane affairs, and whom they try to manage and propitiate and bully for their own advantage; while the trader, on his part, gets to know them so well during this process that he usually gets fond of them, as all white men who really know Africans always do, and looks after them when they are sick or in trouble, and tries to keep them at peace with each other and with the white government, for on peace depends the prosperity that means trade. Therefore, on the whole, the trader knows his African better than all the other sorts of white men put together, and he demonstrates this in two ways. Firstly, he calls upon the gods to be informed why he is condemned to live and deal with such a set of human beings, as those blacks; and then, if the gods remove him from them and send him home to live among white men, he spends the rest of his days contrasting the white and black human beings to the disadvantage of the former, and hankering to get back to the Coast, which demonstrates that the trader feels more than other men the fascination of West Africa, in other words that he understands West Africa, and therefore that he is the person most fitted to speak regarding it, and the most valuable collector of facts that the student of the primitive culture in the region can get to act for him.

I will now turn from presenting you with the credentials of Mr. Dennett to the consideration of the value of these stories which he has sent up to the Folk-Lore Society, and which are laid before you quite untouched by other white hands. Mr. Dennett's own knowledge of the Fjort language has enabled him to give them in a fuller and more connected form than is usually given to the African story.

The position in the native culture of stories, such as those of which you have specimens here, is exceedingly interesting. African native literature (if one may so call it, while it has no native written language) consists of four branches—proverbs, stories, riddles, and songs. Burton, in his *Wit and Wisdom of West Africa*, collected many of the proverbs; and Ellis, in his important works on the Tshi, Ewè, and Yoruba-speaking peoples, has also collected specimens of all of the three first-named classes. So far, I think, no one has dealt with the songs, and indeed it would be exceedingly difficult to do so, as in the songs, more than in any other native thing, as far as I can judge, do you find yourself facing the strange under-meaning in the very words themselves. But, interesting as the songs and riddles are, the proverbs and stories are infinitely the more important portions of the native literature, for in them we get the native speaking to his fellow-native, not to the white man, about his beliefs.

The stories can be roughly divided into three classes (only roughly, because one story will sometimes have material in it belonging to two classes)—legal, historical, and play. You have in this small collection examples of all these. The Nzambi stories are historico-legal; the " Crocodile and the Hen" is legal; "the Wonderful Child " is play-story, and so on.

As a general rule, historical stories are rare among West African tribes; you find more of them among the Fjort than among the Ewé or Tshi * people even, and infinitely more than amongst true forest-belt tribes, like the Ajumba, Fan, and Shekiani. I have repeatedly questioned natives regarding their lack of interest in the past history of their tribes, and have always had the same sort of answer: " Why should we trouble ourselves about that ? They (the dead) lived as we live now. A chief long ago bought, and sold, and fought ; we now buy, and sell, and fight. We are here in this world ; he has gone away." This spirit obtains, of course, only regarding the human experiences of the men who have lived " in the old time."

I well remember being struck with a phrase Dr. Nassau used: " the future which is all around them." Once I asked him why he used it, and he only smiled that grave, half-pitying smile of his ; but as my knowledge of the native grew by experience, I came to understand that phrase, and to put alongside it the phrase: " the past which is all around them." I am afraid a vague make of mind like my own is necessary in order to grasp the African's position ; for every mortal printer who comes across my quotation of the Doctor's phrase puts a long note of interrogation, instantly, in the margin of the proof.

Legal stories, however, do not plunge us into such mental swamps when studying them ; and they are the stories which have the greatest practical value, for in them is contained evidence of the moral code of the African, and a close study of a large number of them gives you a clearer perception of the native ideal of right conduct than any other manifestation of his

* This is the spelling of the word used by Ellis, but it is pronounced by the natives " T'chewhe."

mind that I know of. You will find them all pointing out the same set of lessons : that it is the duty of a man to honour his elders ; to shield and sustain those dependent on him, either by force of hand or by craft; that violence, or oppression, or wrong done can be combated with similar weapons ; that nothing can free a man from those liabilities which are natural to him ; and, finally, that the ideal of law is justice—a cold, hard justice which does not understand the existence of mercy as a thing apart from justice. For example, a man, woman, or child, not knowing what it does, damages the property of another human being. Native justice requires, and contains in itself, that if it can be proved the act was committed in ignorance that was not a culpable ignorance, the doer cannot be punished according to the law. I by no means wish you to think that the administration of the law is perfect, but merely that the underlying principles of the law itself are fairly good.

The part these stories play in the administration of justice is remarkable. They clearly are the equivalents to leading cases with us, and just as the English would cite A v. B, so would the African cite some such story as "The Crocodile and the Hen," or any other stories you find ending with " and the people said it was right." Naturally, the art in pleading lies in citing the proper story for the case—one that either puts your client in the light of a misunderstood, suffering innocent, or your adversary in that of a masquerading villain.

It may at first strike the European as strange, when, listening to the trial of a person for some offence before either a set of elders, or a chief, he observes that the discussion of the affair soon leaves the details of the case itself, and busies itself with the consideration of the conduct of a hyæna and a bush-cat, or the reason why monkeys live in trees, or some such matter; but if the European once gets used to the method, and does not merely request to be informed why he should be expected to play at Æsop's Fables at his time of life, the fascination of the game will seize on him, and he will soon be able to play at Æsop's Fables with the best, and to point out that the case, say, of the Crocodile and the Hen, does not exonerate some friend of a debtor of his from having committed iniquity in not having given up property, lodged with him by the debtor, to its rightful owner.

Regarding the play-stories, it is not necessary for me to speak, they are merely interesting from the scraps of information you find embedded in them regarding native customs and the native way of looking on life.

The form of religion which Mr. Dennett calls Nkissism requires a great deal of attention and study, and seems to me exceedingly interesting, most particularly so in its form in KaCongo and Loango, where, in my opinion, it is an imported religion. I say *my opinion*, merely because I do not wish to involve Mr. Dennett in a statement of which he may disapprove; but you will find Mr. Dennett referring to the manner in which Fumu Kongo, the King of Congo, sent his two sons to take possession of the provinces of KaCongo and Loango, which to this day bear their names, and that he sent with them wise men, learned in the cult of Nzambi, and that at each place whereat the princes stayed they left a Nkiss. I am driven to conjecture that in introducing these Nkissi and their attendant Ngangas, the two princes were introducing a foreign religion into KaCongo and Loango—the religion of their father, the King of Congo. During my own sojourns on the South-West-African Coast, I got to know whereabouts you may expect to meet with the Nkiss and its Nganga, when you are coming down the Coast from the north; and I can only say that I have never been able myself to find, or to find among those people more conversant with the Coast than I am, any trace of the existence of Nkissism until you reach the confines of the kingdom of Loango. It is true, the essential forms of fetish-worship and ideas of Loango, KaCongo and Congo, are common to the districts north of them, namely, the Ogowé, the Cameroons, the Oil Rivers, and the Bight of Benin; yet, if I may so call it, that particular school of fetish called Nkissism you do not meet with until you strike the northern limits of the old kingdom of Kongo.

Where exactly this school of fetish arose I am unable to say, but I think its home, from divers observations made by Sir H. H. Johnston, who has given much attention to the ethnology or the Bantu, must have been the region to the south-east or east-south-east of the region where it was first discovered by Europeans, namely, in the kingdom of Congo. There are many points in it which sharply differentiate it from the form of fetish of the true Negro, and it seems to be the highest form that the fetish of the Bantu has attained to.

We have an enormous amount of information of an exceedingly interesting character left us by the early Portuguese navigators and by the Italian, Portuguese, and Flemish Roman Catholic missionaries who worked so devotedly for nearly 200 years from 1490 in the kingdom of Congo. Yet, so far as I have been able to discover, they give one little, if any, information regarding the traditional history of Congo prior to its discovery by the Portuguese. They found there what they regarded as a prosperous and wealthy state in a condition of considerable

culture, an immense territory ruled over by vassal lords subject
to one king, who was a temporal king, clearly distinct from the
fetish king of the true Negroes. From the accounts they give of
the native religion, which, unfortunately for the ethnologist, they
scorned and detested too much to study in detail, there is little
doubt that that form of religion was Nkissism and that "the
wizards," whom they term Gangas, the chasing whereof gave
the worthy fathers such excellent sport, were no other than the
Nganga Nkissi Mr. Dennett describes.

Regarding, however, the territorial relationship between
Congo and KaCongo and Loango these early historians are yet
more unsatisfactory. The missionaries, however, have occasion
now and then to speak of the natives of the north banks of the
Congo, because they were occasionally cast among them when,
by a turn in the wheel of fortune, the wizards got the upper
hand, or a subsidiary chief to the King of Congo rebelled; and
they always speak of these north-bank people as being fearsome
and savage tribes, given to the eating of men and so on. And
this bad opinion of them was evidently held by the Kongoes
themselves; for it was with direct intent to get two Capuchin
Fathers killed, for example, that the Count of Sogno, during his
rebellion about 1636, drove the Fathers out of his domains. "After
having been much misused and unprovided of all necessaries,
they were left on the confines of the Count's dominions on a
little uninhabited island of the River Zaire.* Here they made
a shift to support themselves two or three days, Father Thomas,
who was the least hurt of the two, going out to hunt for their

* Regarding the islanders of the Lower Congo in 1700, Barbot says:
"They are strong, well-set, live after a beastly manner, and converse
with the Devil." *A Description of the Coasts of North and South Guinea*,
by John Barbot, Agent-General of the Royal Company of Africa and the
Islands of America, at Paris, 1732.

subsistence. But at length they were unexpectedly delivered from thence by some pagan fishermen, who took them on board and carried them to a city of theirs called Bombangoij, in the kingdom of Angoy.*   Here, arriving at night, they were very courteously entertained by an infidel of the place, who gave them supper and, moreover, assigned to them a house and three women to wait on them after the manner of the country.   But our Fathers, not caring to trust themselves among these people, soon after they had supped, sending away their women, meditated an escape.   For this purpose Father Thomas, who was the best able to walk, took his lame companion on his back and marched out of the house ; but before he had gone far, he was forced through weakness to set down his burden under a great shady tree, which, as soon as day appeared, for fear of discovery they got up into.   Their patron, coming that morning to visit his guests and finding them gone, much wondered, and well knowing they could not go far by reason of the condition he left them in, immediately went about to search after them.   Coming at last near the place where they were, and not having yet found them, a pagan thought came into his head that they might have been carried away by some spirit, which he expressed after this manner : ' If the devil has carried them away, I suppose he did it that they might make me no recompense for my kindness.'   Our Fathers, hearing this, could not forbear laughing, even amidst their miseries and misfortunes, and putting out their

---

* Merolla says : "Angoij is a kingdom rather in name than in dominion, having but a small territory.   Here, formerly, a certain *Mani*, happening to marry a mulatto, daughter to a very rich Portuguese, his father-in-law would needs make him King of Angoij, and for this purpose caused him to rebel against the King of Kacongo, his lawful lord."   Angoij was a small territory on the seaward end of the north bank of the Congo.

heads from the tree, cried out: 'We are here, friend, never doubt our gratitude ; for we only went out of the house to refresh ourselves with the rays of the morning sun.' Hereat the old man, being exceedingly rejoiced, immediately took them down, and putting them into two nets (hammocks) sent them away to Capinda (Kabinda), a port in the kingdom of Angoij, about two days from Bombangoij."*

This account, I think, shows clearly that in 1636 Loango and KaCongo were not provinces of the king of Congo, for had they been so, the Capuchins would have had no dread of the inhabitants, but have known they were safe; for, although they were driven out of Sogno, this had been done entirely because they were Capuchins. The Count of Sogno immediately attempted to supply their place with Franciscans, his objection to Capuchins arising from his regarding them as allies of the Portuguese and King of Kongo, against whom he was at war; and, although it may be urged that the early missionaries to Congo were in the habit of going up trees, some of them, indeed cautiously bringing out with them from home rope-ladders for that purpose, yet this is the only instance, I think, of their climbing up them out of the way of natives. The usual cause was an "exceeding plentie of lions and tygers and other monsters, for not half of which," they cheerily observed, "would they have made a mouthful."

Proyart gives us a slightly more definite statement. He says :—"The King of Congo claims the Kingdom of KaCongo as a province of his States, and the King of KaCongo, doubtless

---

* *A Voyage to Congo*, by Father Jerome Merolla da Sorrento, 1682. *Churchill Collection*, vol. i. p. 521.

by way of reprisals, never calls himself any other title but Ma Congo, King of Congo, instead of King of KaCongo, a title given him by foreigners, and one that suits him. These pretensions are not always unfounded; many small kingdoms of savage states, which at the present day share Africa among them, were originally provinces dependent on other kingdoms, the particular governors of which usurped the sovereignty. It is not long since Sogno ceased to be a province of the kingdom of Congo."*

Unfortunately there is no means of fixing any date to the severance of the two north-bank provinces from the main kingdom. Apparently they had asserted their independence long enough for the question not to have been a burning political one in Congo at the time of Diego Caõ's discovery of the Congo in 1484. It is, however, idle to conjecture how long prior to that date KaCongo and Loango ceased to be fiefs of the King of Congo. It may have been centuries, or it may have been but a few decades; for, for some time prior to Diego Caõ's arrival, Congo itself had been so terribly worried by those interesting, but, as yet, undetermined people, the Gagas or Gindes (a fearful, warlike, cannibal tribe, who, according to Battel,† who was amongst them about 1595, came from Sierra Leone, harassed the inland borders of Congo and penetrated as far south as Dondo in Angola) that, at the time of the coming of Diego Caõ, undoubtedly the public mind was entirely concentrated on these Gagas—a condition of affairs which enabled the Portuguese and their missionaries to obtain the ascendancy in

---

* *History of Loango and Kacongo*, by the Abbé Proyart. Paris, 1776.

† *The Strange Adventures of Andrew Battel of Leigh in Essex.* (Purchas His Pilgrims.) See also *A Curious and Exact Account of a Voyage to Congo in the years 1666 and 1667*, by Michael Angelo of Gattina and Denis de Carli of Piacenza. 1723. *Churchill Collection.*

c

the kingdom, as they did, and which would, in all human probability but for their timely arrival, have wiped the kingdom of Congo out.

This distraction was sufficiently great to have caused a people so deficient in interest in historical matters to have almost forgotten the severance from the main kingdom (which was situated on the southern bank of the Great River) of two provinces on the northern bank, even had the severance been comparatively recent—provinces, moreover, that could never have been much in touch with the throne-town at San Salvador on account of their difficulty of access, the terrific current of the river making canoe-journeys across its stream alike difficult and dangerous.

But a far stronger proof than there is in the scattered observations relating to the affair in white literature, of the tradition of the two sons of Fumu Kongo, as given by Mr. Dennett, being a historical tradition, I think is found in the existence in KaCongo and Loango of this peculiar form of fetish, Nkissism. It is surrounded in these provinces on all sides, save the sea and the Congo, by a dissimilar form of fetish, which I believe to be the form of fetish Nkissism supplanted.

During my first visit to Africa I came in contact with the Fjort tribes and learnt much from Mr. Dennett personally regarding their beliefs and customs; and all that I myself saw fully bore out the accuracy of his statements about them. During my second visit my time was mainly spent among tribes inhabiting country to the north and north-east of the Fjorts, and among those tribes I did not find the Nkiss and Nganga as aforesaid. Nevertheless, I found something extremely like some of the Nkiss of the Fjorts: deities which, as far as I can see from observations on their powers and spheres of influence, are simply indistinguishable from some of the Nkiss which Mr. Dennett describes as acknowledged among the Fjort, such ones as that of the Mountain Mungo. This sort of deity is called by the Mpongwe-speaking tribes *Ombuiri*. They have, however, no priesthood whatsoever attached to their service. Every human being who passes one of their places of habitation has to do obeisance to the Ombuiri who inhabits it, just to give some trifling object in homage as a token of respect. As a general rule the Imbuiri (pl.) are, as West African deities go, fairly inoffensive; but now and then one will rise up and kill someone by throwing down a tree on a passer by its forest glade, or, by swelling up the river it resides in, will cause devastating inundation. But it is really quite a different species of deity from the regular Nkiss, such as was introduced by the emissaries of Fumu Kongo into the regions of KaCongo and Loango. You would never, for example, if you were a member of a Mpongwe stem tribe, think of calling in an Ombuiri to settle the question of who killed a man or who had stolen something. You would call in a totally different class of spirit. Yet when you are in KaCongo or Loango, or among the Ivili tribe,* you will see these great, honourable, ancient Nature-spirits, these Imbuiri themselves, in charge of a mere human priest employed in the most trivial affairs concerning thefts of garden hoes or cooking-pots and such like; and I am quite sure, if you have a Mpongwe soul in you, you will be deeply shocked at this degradation. If

---

* A small and dying-out set of Fjorts, living in a few villages near the confluence of the Ogowe-Okanda and the Ngunie Rivers, having a tradition that they came from Loango and were driven by bad weather into the Ogowe and by bad men to their present situation.

you were only an ethnologist, ignorant of the little bit of history regarding the King of Congo and the Nganga he sent with his Nkissi from his throne-town of San Salvador into the conquered provinces of KaCongo, Loango and Ngoio, you might be tempted to regard an Ombuiri having a priest and a ritual of a definite kind attached to it, as an instance of a development in religious thought and a demonstration of how gods at large are made. But with a knowledge of the history of the affair, dateless as that history is, I think you will be induced to believe that the Imbuiri have merely suffered that change which nature-spirits have suffered in other lands taken possession of by a conqueror with a religion of his own: namely, that some of the spirits worshipped by the conquered people were held in such respect that the conquerors held it more politic to adopt them into their own religion, after making suitable alterations in their characters, than to attempt to destroy them; and so it is that to-day you will find Imbuiri made into Nkissi and existing in esteem and worship side by side with a very different kind of deity, the true Nkissi of Fumu Kongo.

The best authority for the present condition of the Fjort religion is Monteiro, who says: " In times past the King of Congo was very powerful. All the country, as far as and including Loanda, the River Congo and Cabinda, was subject to him and paid him tribute. The missionaries under his protection worked far and wide, attained great riches, and were of immense benefit to the country, where they and the Portuguese established and fostered sugar-cane plantations, indigo manufactories, iron-smelting and other kindred trades. With the discovery and colonisation of the Brazils, however, and the expulsion of the Jesuits from Angola, the power of the Portuguese and of the King of Congo has dwindled away to its present miserable condition. The King of Congo is now only Chief of San Salvador and a few other small towns, and does not receive the least tribute from any other, nor does he possess any power in the land. Among the natives of Angola, however, he still retains a certain amount of prestige as King of Congo, and all would do homage to him in his presence, as he is considered to possess the greatest fetish of all the kings and tribes, though powerless to exact tribute from them." *

Things are to-day exactly as Monteiro describes them regarding the natives. KaCongo is under Portuguese rule, Loango under French; the regions that were part of the old main kingdom are divided between Portugal and Congo Belge. But the natives of these countries alike acknowledge the importance of the King of Congo's fetish, while just north of Loango you meet with the regions of the tribes that regard him not; they may have heard of him, but his fetish is not their fetish, for they never fell under the rule of Nkissi.

I need now only detain you with a few remarks about the infusion of Christian doctrine into the original Fjort fetish. The admixture of doctrines both from Christian missionary teaching, and from Mohammedan, makes the study of the real form of the native's own religion difficult in several West African districts, notably so at Sierra Leone, the Gold, Slave, and Ivory coasts, and among the Fjort of the Congo and Angola. But, provided you are acquainted with the forms of fetish in districts which have not been under white influence, such as those of the great forest-belt from the Niger to the

---

* *Angola and the River Congo*, by J. J. Monteiro. Macmillan, 1875.

Niari, a little care will enable you to detect what is, and what is not, purely native.

It is true that the whole of the Fjorts were under the sway of Roman Catholicism more thoroughly and for a greater duration of time than any other West African people have been under any European influence. The energy with which the kings of Congo took it up from the first was remarkable, but it is open to doubt whether those dusky monarchs were not in so doing as much actuated by temporal considerations as spiritual. As I have mentioned before, when the Portuguese first came into the country, the country was in imminent peril from the Gagas, a peril from which the Portugese rescued it. The whole aim of the Congoese thereupon became to be as much like the Portuguese as possible. Many natives went up to Lisbon and were received with great courtesy by the king, João II.; and while there they saw, in the keen but empirical African native way, how great a veneration the Portuguese held their priests in, how the very king himself did them homage, and how even ships durst hardly leave haven on a voyage without a chaplain on board. And there is little doubt that from these observations the Congoese regarded the Roman Catholic priests with great veneration, and thought that in them and their teaching lay the secret of earthly power, at any rate; and the king of Congo and his subsidiary princes did their utmost to get as many of these priests to come and live among them and instruct them as possible, and when there the priests themselves, by their own nobility, devotion, and courage, confirmed the Congoese in their opinion of their, to them, superhuman powers. Ceaselessly active, regardless of danger, they led armies into battle, and notably into that great battle in which Alfonso I. of Congo, the

Christianised king, fought with his brother, Pasanquitama, for the crown, and had his army saved from immolation and given victory by the appearance of St. James and an angelic host fighting on his side in the crisis of the battle.

It is impossible in the space at my command to enter into the history of the Roman Catholic mission to Congo, owing to its great complexity of detail. Capuchins, Jesuits, Franciscans alike laboured there; but the doctrine they taught being uniformly that of Rome, it affords no such difficulty in recognition among the native traditions as do the results of the other forms of Christian mission. Moreover, the hold of the missionaries was not by any means so great in KaCongo and Loango as it was in the kingdom of Congo itself. Merolla says: "The kingdom of Loango lies in 5° and a half, south latitude. The Christian religion was first planted there in the year 1663,* by the labour and diligence of one Father Ungaro, a friar of our Order. Father Bernardino Ungaro, on entering into his work of evangelising Loango, commenced by baptising the king and queen, after having instructed them for some days, and then marrying them according to the manner of our church. His next business was to baptise the king's eldest son, and after him, successively, the whole court, which consisted of about 300 persons. In a word, within the space of a year that he lived there he had baptised upwards of 12,000 people. At last this zealous missioner, finding himself oppressed by a grievous indisposition and believing that he should not live long, sent for our lay Brother Leonard, who coming not long after to him, the pious

---

* One hundred and sixty-seven years later than in Congo, and therefore at the time of the breaking up of the Portuguese power by the Dutch, who are referred to by the missionaries as "the Heretics."

father died the same morning that he arrived, well provided, as
we may imagine, of merits for another world.

"The good king hearing this, and being desirous to keep up
what he had so happily begun, sent Brother Leonard to the
aforesaid Superior (Father João Maria de Pavia in Angola) to
acquaint him with Ungaro's death and to desire him to speedily
send another missioner; but, however, these his good intentions
were afterwards disappointed by a rebellion raised against him
by a kinsman, who, being ambitious of his crown, and having
been assisted by some apostate Catholics, deprived the good king
of his life. The tyrant and usurper that dispossessed him lived
not long after to enjoy his ill-gotten throne, but was snatched
away from it by a sudden death. This wicked person being
dead, another king arose, who, though he did all he could by
the help of one Capuchin, to promote what had been begun by
Father Ungaro, yet was not able to bring his intentions about,
and that for want of more missioners, wherefore the kingdom
remains at present, as formerly, buried in idolatry. In my time
were several attempts made to recover our interest there, though
to no purpose. . . . . . I never heard there was any Christian
prince in the kingdom of Angoij (Cabinda), that country having
been always inhabited by a sort of people extremely given to
sorcery and magic." *

There is yet another passage in Merolla's very wise and
very charming work that has an especial bearing on the subjects
treated of in this book of Mr. Dennett's. The holy Father gives
a long list of "the abuses" existing in his time among the

---

* *A Voyage to Congo*, by Father Jerome Merolla da Sorrento, 1682.
Churchill Collection, vol. i.

natives of Kongo. This list has a double interest. It shows us how acute a mind he had, how clearly he saw the things that were fundamental to the form of religion he battled against; but it has a great interest to an ethnologist apart from this, as it gives us a clearer insight into native custom than has been given us by any subsequent traveller in that region, and moreover because there is not one custom that the holy Father classes as "an abuse " that does not exist to-day with the same force as in the seventeenth century. I will only detain you now with Merolla's description of " The seventh abuse," that of prohibited foods, for you will often in this book come across references by Mr. Dennett to the Kazila.

" Seventhly, it is the custom that either the parents or the wizards give certain rules to be inviolably observed by the young people, and which they call Chegilla. These were to abstain from eating either some sorts of poultry, the flesh of some kinds of wild beasts, such and such fruits ; roots either raw or boiled after this or another manner, with several other ridiculous injunctions of the like nature, too many to be enumerated here. You would wonder with what religious observance these in- junctions were obeyed. These young people would sooner chuse to fast several days together than to taste the least bit of what has been forbidden them ; and if it sometime happen that the Chegilla has been neglected to have been given them by their parents, they think they shall presently die unless they go to receive it from the wizards. A certain young Negro being upon a journey lodged in a friend's house by the way; his friend, before he went out the next morning, had got a wild hen ready for his breakfast, they being much better than tame ones. The Negro hereupon demanded, 'If it were a wild hen?' His host answered, 'No.' Then he fell on heartily and afterwards proceeded on his journey. After four years these two met together again, and the aforesaid Negro being not yet married, his old friend asked him, 'If he would eat a wild hen,' to which he answered, 'That he had received his Chegilla and could not.' Hereat the host began immediately to laugh, inquiring of him, 'What made him refuse it now, when he had eaten one at his table about four years ago?' At the hearing of this the Negro immediately fell a trembling, and suffered himself to be so far possessed with the effects of imagination, that he died in less than twenty-four hours after." *

The subject of these prohibitions regarding either some particular form of food, or some particular manner of eating any form of food, is a very interesting one.

You will find in West Africa, under all the various schools of fetish thought, among both Negro and Bantu, that every individual, slave or free, so long as he is not under either European or Mahommedan influence, has a law that there is some one thing that he individually may not do. Among the Calabar people it is called Ibet, which signifies a command, a law, an abstinence. Among the Gaboon people it is called Orunda, which Dr. Nassau informs me signifies a prohibition. Among the Fjorts it is called Kecheela or Chegilla. But under whatever name you meet it, it is in itself always the same in its essential character, for it is always a prohibition regarding food.

* *A Voyage to Congo*, by Father Jerome Merolla da Sorrento, 1682. *Churchill Collection*, vol. i. p. 237.

When I was in West Africa in daily contact with this custom and the inconveniences it presents, like any prohibition custom, to every-day affairs, I endeavoured to collect information regarding it. At first I thought it might be connected with the totemism I had read of; but I abandoned this view, finding no evidence to support it, and much that went against it.

Sometimes I found that one prohibition would be common to a whole family regarding some particular form of food; but the individual members of that family had each an individual prohibition apart from the family one. Moreover, there was always a story to account for the whole family abstaining from eating some particular animal. That animal had always afforded signal help to the family, or its representative, at some crisis in life. I never came across, as I expected to, a story of the family having descended from the animal in question, nor for the matter of that any animal whatsoever; and these stories regarding the help received from animals which caused the family in gratitude to avoid killing them were always told voluntarily and openly. There was not the touch of secrecy and mystery that lurks round the reason of the Ibet or Orunda. Therefore I rather doubt whether these prohibitions common to an entire family are identical with the true Orunda, Ibet, or Kecheela.

Mr. Dennett in his chapter on *The Folklore of the Fjort,* evidently referring to this eating of his Kecheela, says that "so long as he knows nothing about it, the Fjort may eat out of unclean pots, but if he knows that anything unclean has been cooked in the pot in which his food has been prepared, and he eats thereof, he will be punished by some great sickness coming over him, or by death."

I am unable, from my own experience, to agree with this statement that ignorance would save the man who had eaten his prohibited food. From what I know, Merolla's story as cited above is the correct thing : the man, though he eat in ignorance, dies or suffers severely.

It is true that one of the doctrines of African human law is that the person who offends in ignorance, that is not a culpable ignorance, cannot be punished ; but this merciful dictum I have never found in spirit-law. Therein if you offend, you suffer ; unless you can appease the enraged spirit, neither ignorance nor intoxication is a feasible plea in extenuation. Therefore I think that Mr. Dennett's informant in this case must have been a man of lax religious principles ; and in Merolla's story I feel nearly certain that the man who gives his friend his Chegilla to eat must have been one of the holy Father's converts, engaged in trying to break down the superstition of his fellow-country-man. Had he been a believer in Chegilla himself, he would have known that the outraged spirit of the Chegilla would have visited its wrath on him, as well as on his friend, with a fine impartiality and horrible consequences.

The inevitableness of spirit-vengeance, unless suitable sacrifices are made, seems to me also demonstrated in another way. Poisoning is a thing much dreaded in West Africa ; practically it is a dread that overshadows every man's life there. I personally doubt whether white people are poisoned so frequently as is currently supposed in West Africa. But undoubtedly it is practised among the natives ; and the thing that holds it in reasonable check is the virulence of the attack made on the poisoner, or, as the poisoner is currently called, the witch. Briefly, poisoning is the most common form of witchcraft in West Africa. The witch has other methods of destroying the victims—catching their souls, witching young crocodiles, &c., into them—but poisoning is the sheet-anchor, and is regarded on the same lines as soul-theft, &c. Now there is one form of poisoning which is regarded among all the various tribes I know as a particularly vile one ; and that is giving a person a prohibited food. For example, to give a man, whose Orunda is boiled chicken, a mess containing boiled chicken, or to boil a chicken and take it from the pot and then cook his meal in the pot, is equivalent to giving him so much prussic acid or strychnine. But in spite of its efficacy in destroying an enemy, this giving of the prohibited food is re-garded as a very rare form of the crime of poisoning, because of the great danger to himself the giver would incur from the wrath of the spirit to whom the prohibited food belonged. The great iniquity of this form of the crime of poisoning, I believe, lies in its injuring, in some way, the soul of the victim after death.

. Mr. Dennett, moreover, in the passage I have quoted uses the word " unclean." He does this from his habit of using scriptural phraseology ; but I entirely disapprove of the use of the word " unclean " in connection with these Ibet. Orunda or Kecheela matters should suggest the word consecrated, or sacrificed, to be substituted. The West African has a whole series of things he abstains from doing, or from touching, because he believes them truly to be unclean. For example, he regards the drinking of milk from animals as a filthy practice, and also the eating of eggs ; and he will ask why you use these forms of animal excreta and avoid the others. And there are several other things besides that he regards as loathsome in themselves. But there is nothing loathsome or unclean in things connected with this prohibited food. There are, I believe, and I think I may say Dr. Nassau would support me in this view, things that a man dedicates for the whole of his natural life to the use of his individual attendant guardian spirit.

This Roman Catholic influence over the Fjort may, I think, be taken as having been an evanescent one. I do not say, as the Rev. J. Leighton Wilson does, that this is so, because Roman Catholicism is an unfit means of converting Africans; but it suffered the common fate that has so far overtaken all kinds of attempts to Europeanise the African. It is like cutting a path in one of their native forests. You may make it a very nice path—a clean, tidy, and good one—but if you leave it, it grows over again, and in a few seasons is almost indistinguishable from the surrounding bush. The path the Roman Catholics made was one intended to lead the African to Heaven. At first, the African thought it was to lead him to earthly power and glory and riches. During the ascendancy of the Portuguese in the region it did this; but when their power was crippled, it did not. Therefore the African "let it go for bush"; and it is his blame, not the missionary's, that the Fjort to-day is found by Europeans in a state of culture lower than many African tribes, and with a religion as dependent " on conversing with the Devil " as ever— in short, a very interesting person to the folklorist.

The mind of the African has a wonderful power of assimilating other forms of belief apart from fetish; and when he has had a foreign idea put into his mind it remains there, gradually taking on to itself a fetish form; for the fetish idea overmasters it, so long as the foreign idea is left without reinforcements, and it becomes a sort of fossil. The teachings of the Roman Catholic missionaries are now in this fossil state in the mind of the Fjort. Ardent ethnologists may wish that they had never been introduced ; but it is well to remember that their religion was not the only thing introduced into the region by them, for the Fjort of to-day owes almost all his food supply to them : the maize, the mango, the banana, and most likely the manioc. Nevertheless the high intelligence of the Fjort, as evidenced by their having, before coming into contact with Europeans, an organised state of society, a definitely thought-out religion, and an art superior to that of all other Bantu West Coast tribes, makes them a tribe that the student of the African cannot afford to ignore, because the study of them entails a little trouble and a knowledge of the doctrine taught by the Roman Catholic Church.

MARY H. KINGSLEY.

Mr. Dennett on reading the proofs of the foregoing introduction, and in response to an invitation from me for any suggestions, sent a number of notes. I select from these for insertion here such as relate to historical and ethnological questions ; the rest will be more appropriately placed in Appendix I.

p. xix. " Miss Kingsley mentions a lost part of the Loango race (Bavili) in the Ogowe, and calls them Ivili (singular). *Vila* is to lose, in Fjort. Thus, the Bavili were the lost men, lost in their journey northward."

p. xx. " The only Fumu was Kongo, king of the united provinces. He sent his sons under the title of Mafumu to rule these provinces. They in their turn divided their lands among their children under the title of Tekklifumu. To-day, Fumu has come to mean chief, head of a family ; it really means Judge.

The son in Manifumu, the grandson, Tekklifumu. *Ma* is short for *Mani* (son of); so that MaKongo simply meant son of Kongo; and it is a proof that MaKongo always recognised his secondary position, just as MaLoango does today. KaCongo should probably be written KaciKongo, which would give the sense of Middle Kongo.

" Ngoio was the name of the great Rain-doctor sent with Ma-Kongo and MaLoango, by Fumu Kongo; and he gave his name to the province he took possession of, like MaKongo and Ma-Loango did; and not only to the province, but to the chieftain-ship of it. Strange to say, to this day Ncanlam, the chief of the Musurongo, has the right to take the cap (*succeed to the chief-tainship of the province Ngoio*); but as Ngoio (*the chief of this province*) is always killed the day after he takes the cap, the throne remains vacant "—*i.e. no one likes to lose his life for a few hours' glory on the Ngoio throne.*

The italics are mine.

M. H. K.

NOTES ON THE FOLKLORE OF THE FJORT.

I.

THE FOLKLORE OF THE FJORT.

By the Fjort I mean the tribes that once formed the great kingdom of Congo. From the Quillo river, north of Loango, to the River Logo, south of Kinsembo, on the south-west coast of Africa, and as far almost as Stanley Pool in the interior, this kingdom is said to have extended. My remarks refer chiefly to the KaCongo and Loango provinces: that is to say, to the two coast provinces north of the great river Congo or Zaire.

The religion or superstition of the Fjort, as well as their laws, can easily be traced to their source, namely, to San Salvador, the headquarters or capital of the great Fumu Kongo. Their legends describe how Fumu Kongo sent his sons Ka-Congo and Loango to govern these provinces; and their route can be traced by their having left what you call fetishes at each place where they slept.* These fetishes are called Nkissi nsi, the spirit or mystery of the earth, just as the ruler or nFumu

---

* See my *Seven Years among the Fjort.* London, 1887, p. 50, *sqq.*

B

is called Fumu nsi, the prince of the land or earth. Together
with these two sons of Kongo (called Muene nFumu, or, as we
should write it, *Manifumu*), the king sent a priest or rain-
doctor, called Ngoio. Even to this day, when the rains do
not come in their proper season, the princes of KaCongo and
Loango send ambassadors to Cabinda or Ngoio with presents
to the rain-doctor, or, as they call him, Nganga.

Loango, KaCongo, and Ngoio are now all spoken of as
nFumu nsi ; and their existence is admitted, although, as a
matter of fact, their thrones are vacant, and each petty prince,
or head of a family, governs his own little town or towns.
Each little town or collection of towns, or better perhaps each
family, has now its patch of ground sacred to the spirit of the
earth (Nkissi nsi),* its Nganga nsi, the head of the family, and
its Nganga Nkissi (charm or fetish doctor), and its Nganga bilongo (medicine-doctor or surgeon). Nzambi-Mpungu is what
we should call the Creator. Nzambi (wrongly called God) is
Mother Earth, literally Terrible Earth. In all the Fjort legends
that treat of Nzambi she is spoken of as the " mother," generally of a beautiful daughter, or as a great princess calling all
the animals about her to some great meeting, or palaver ; or as
a poor woman carrying a thirsty or hungry infant on her back,
begging for food, who then reveals herself and punishes those

* Thus the voyage of Kongo's sons KaCongo and Loango from San
Salvador to Loango is marked for us ; for where they rested the ground
became blessed (Nkissiansi, land sacred to the spiritual law family Fetish).
There are no altars made with hands, no images among the Nkissiansi.
Sometimes one meets with a stone, a mound of earth, a tree, a mound
of shells, on this holy ground, and I have met with huts containing the
family fetishes

who refused her drink or food by drowning them,* or by re-
warding with great and rich presents those who have given her
child drink. Animals and people refer their palavers to her
as judge. Her name also is used as an ejaculation.

Nkissi nsi is the mysterious spirit that dwells in the earth.
Nkissi is the mysterious power in herbs, medicines, fetishes.

The missionary is called a Nganga Nzambi. This alone proves,
I think, that the natives consider Nzambi, the earth, as their
deity; and when once the missionaries are convinced of this
fact it should be their duty to protest against the use of the
word Nzambi as the equivalent to the white man's God. The
word they must use is Nzambi Mpungu, or perhaps they had
better make a new word. Mpungu, or mpoungou, is the word
used by the Fjort to mean gorilla. This should delight the
heart of the evolutionist. But *mpounga* has the signification of
something that covers. There are, however, no gorillas south
of the Congo, and in the Ntandu dialect mpoungou has the
signification of *creator* or *father*. And we must remember that
this religion came from the south of the Congo.

Upon the sacred earth in each village or family a small hut
or shimbec is usually built, where the family fetish is kept. A
tree is also usually planted there, and holes are made in it,
where medicines are placed. Each hole is then covered by a
piece of looking glass, which is kept in its place by a rim of clay,
which again is spluttered over with white and red earth or
chalk, moistened in the mouth of the prince. Here the prince
summons his family to what they call a "washing-up." That
is, after having made their offerings (generally of white fowls)

* *See* below, p. 121.

the people cut the grass and clean up the sacred ground and dance and sing. The prince also on certain occasions admits the young men who have been circumcised to the rights of manhood, and teaches them the secret words which act as pass-words throughout the tribe. The prince is crowned here ; and it is this fetish that he consults whenever he is in trouble.

The Nganga Nkissi has his hut apart from his holy ground ; and there he keeps his image, into which nails, spear-points, knives, etc., are driven by the suppliant who seeks the help of the mysterious spirit to kill his enemies or to protect him against any evil. The Nganga Nkissi also sells charms, such as little wooden images charged with medicines, bracelets, armlets, head-bands, waistbands, little bits of tiger's skin to keep the small-pox away, the little horns of kids, and other pendants for the necklace.

The Nganga bilongo is the doctor and surgeon. Each surgeon or doctor keeps the secret of his cure in the family, so that the sick have sometimes to travel great distances to be cured of certain diseases. After most sicknesses or misfortunes the native undergoes a kind of thanksgiving and purification according to the rites of Bingo, who has a Nganga in almost every family. This is not the same as the form of going through the " paint-house."

The Nkissi, the spirit, as it were, of mother earth, is met with in mountains and rocks. Thus, in the creek that flows behind Ponta da Lenha in the River Congo there is a rock falling straight down into the water, which the natives fear to pass at night ; and even in the daytime they keep close to the far side of the creek. They declare that the Nkissi will swallow them up. The story of the four young men who left their town early in the morning to visit their lovers across the mountains, and after a long visit at about four o'clock wished to return, proves the power of the terrible spirit of the earth. For their lovers determined to see the four young men part of the way home, and so went with them up the mountain. Then the young men saw the young women back to their town. The young women again went up the hill with their lovers, and again the young men came back with them. The earth-spirit got vexed at such levity and turned them all into pillars of clay, as can be proved, for are not the eight pillars visible to this day (white-ant pillars taking the shape of four men and four women)? And the lying woman who said she had no peas for sale when she had her basket full of them, did not the earth-spirit turn her into a pillar of clay, as can be seen in the woods near Cabinda behind Futilla even to this day?

The mountain Mongo is spoken of at times as a person, as in the story of the old lady who, after many exchanges, secured a drum in exchange for the red wood she had given the image-maker, to keep for her. For the old lady took this drum to Mongo and played upon it until Mongo broke it. But she wept and Mongo was sorry for her and gave her some mushrooms and told her to go away.

Islands in the River Congo are spoken of as the home of the men who turn themselves into crocodiles, so that they may upset canoes and drag their prisoners to them and eventually sell them. Monkey Island, just above Boma, in the River Congo, is used as the burial-place of princes of that part of the country.

The names of the rivers are also the names of the spirits of the same. These spirits, like those of the Chimpanzu and

Mlomvu, kill those who drink their waters; others get angry, and swell, and overflow their banks like the Lulondo, and drown many people; while some punish those who fish in their waters for greediness by causing them to become deaf and dumb, as Sunga did in one of the stories I have given on a subsequent page.

Then the great Chamma (rainbow) is described as a huge snake that enters rivers at their source and swells them up, and carries everything before it, grass, trees, at times whole villages, in its way to the sea.

Any place, either in the hills or along the banks of rivers (near fishing places), or near wells, can be reserved by any one by his placing shells, strips of cloth, or other charms there. The nearest approach that we have to these charms in England is the scarecrow, or the hat which the Member of Parliament leaves on his seat to show that the place is his.

The dead bodies of witches are either thrown down precipices or into the rivers.

The sun, Ntangu, and moon, Ngonde, are generally described as two brothers. There is a legend which tells us that two brothers, Ntangu and Ngonde, lived in a village by the sea; and Ntangu bet Ngonde that he could not catch him up, so they set off racing. Ngonde caught up Ntangu; and then Ntangu got vexed and said he could catch up Ngonde, but he never did, so Ngonde won the bet. The fact of the moon's being seen during the day, together with the sun, and the sun's never being seen at night in company with the moon has, no doubt, given rise to this story. I have also collected two versions of a story of two brothers setting out, one after the other, to the land whence no man returns, which also are sun-myths.

I have heard very little about the stars. The new moon is greeted with a cry of " Lu lu lu lu," in a high key, the native beating his mouth with his hand as he cries.

Lightning is said to be made by a blacksmith (Funzi) who lives in the centre of KaCongo. Nzassi means thunder; Lu siemo, lightning; and they are both spoken of as persons, Nzassi being used often for both thunder and lightning. Thus, they say that if it comes on to rain when you are in the woods, and it thunders, and you try to run away, Nzassi runs after you and kills you.

A man named Antonio one day told me a story of how he had seen Nzassi's dogs. It was raining, he declared; and he and his companions were under a shed playing at marbles when it began to thunder and lighten. It thundered frightfully ; and Nzassi sent his twenty-four dogs down upon them. They seized one of the party who had left the shed for a moment, and the fire burnt up a living palm tree.

The sky is spoken of in certain stories as something to be bored through, as in the story where Nzambi on earth promises her beautiful daughter in marriage to anyone who should go to Nzambi above, and bring down a little of Nzambi Mpungu's fire from heaven. The woodpecker bores the hole through which all those anxious to compete for Nzambi's daughter's hand creep, after having climbed up the silken cord made by the spider from heaven to earth.*

The clouds they call Ituti, or rather Matuti (pl.). They rise from where the walls of heaven touch the earth, and sail across the sky to the other side, or round and round about.

---

* The story is given at length on p. 74.

The Fjort divide the year into two seasons: i mûna ki mvula (rainy season), i muna ki sifu (dry season). They divide the month (ngonde) into seven weeks of four days; Tono, Silu, Nkandu, Nsona, on the last of which they do no work.

The sea is known as Mbu. The sun rises in the Mayomba bush-country, and sets in the Mbu.

Before going to sea, the fishermen knock their fetishes to bring them good luck, or to kill those who spoil their luck. If a fisherman goes to sleep, and while he sleeps the little black bird called *ntieti* comes and rests in the stern of his canoe, and in the morning he awakes and finds it there, he knows some misfortune has come upon his family, or is to come upon himself.

The spirit that dwells in the sea is called Chicamassi-chibuinji. At times she comes ashore to collect red-wood and other necessary articles of toilet. Now, when anyone steals some of these articles she gets vexed and causes a calemma (swell) to arise, which stops all fishing and at times causes loss of life to those passing through the surf.

Waterspouts they call *Nvussuko* and *Ngo-lo*; and they fear them as we should a ghost.

They say that they do not make sacrifices to the sea; but that when Chicamassi is vexed she comes ashore and takes one of twins or triplets, and drowns it in the sea. It is well to save a relation from drowning; and if you like to save a stranger's life, he becomes your slave, or gives you a slave in exchange. When the native passes certain places where Chicamassi is supposed to have passed, he throws bits of fish, mandioca, or whatnot, into the sea for her. They also splutter rum into the sea before drinking it.

The tides are caused by Nzambi Mpungu, who, when the time comes, drops a large stone into the ocean to make the water rise, and takes it out again when it is time for low tide.

Zimini has towns under the sand in the sea; and at times he comes up and seizes a man or woman, and takes him or her down to his place. There are stories in which the white man is said to have his town under the sea, and to take thither all the slaves he captures and buys to help him to make his cloth.

Woods and forests are the homes of the Mpunia (highway robber and murderer), Ndotchi (witch), and Chimbindi (spirit of the departed).

The Nkissi that exists in herbs, plants, and trees, poisons or cures people; and the natives have a great knowledge of the different properties of plants, herbs, and trees. The Nkissi grows with the plant out of the earth.

Fetishes are made of a wood called Mlimbe; and it is said that when the tree is felled the blood that flows from the tree is mixed with the blood of a cock that the Nganga kills. This cock used to be a slave, when slaves were cheaper than they are now.

Grasses are worn as charms around the neck or body of a sick man.

The greater number of natives are called after animals. Ngo, the leopard; Nkossa, the lobster; Chingumba, lion; Nzau, elephant; Memvu, a kind of wild dog; are the names given those of royal blood; and the greatest of these names is that of Ngo. Only princes can wear a leopard's skin. The Leopard, the royal animal, the figure of royal motherhood (the earth, as opposed to Nkala, the crab, the figure of the sea), is the name given to women through whom the royal line may descend, Kongo being the name of the Fjort's Adam, the great and first King or Nfumu (judge), the father of KaCongo and Loango and Ngoio. And many customs touching the hunting and slaying of the Leopard still exist, and in themselves would form an interesting study. Its skin is still worn as a sign of Royalty, and its hair is used as a charm against small pox : thirty skins used to be sent from Loango to Ngoio, so that he might send Mbunzi with rain to water his plantations.

In listening to their many stories about animals, one forgets for the time that the relator is talking about animals; and when it comes to where one eats the other, one wonders whether the native forgets that his ancestors did act in this outrageous fashion. The Fjort believe that some people have the power, or misfortune, to change themselves into beasts of prey, such as leopards and crocodiles. Stories of quite recent date tell of relations who have suffered in this way, and who in their better moods have admitted that they have killed so and so, and torn him to pieces.

This brings us to another interesting subject, that of the kazilas, or things forbidden. Some families, especially those of royal descent, may not eat pig ; others may not touch goat, flat-fish, shell-fish, doves. None except witches would attempt to eat snakes, crocodiles, lizards, chamelions. Many families will not touch certain animals because their ancestors owe such animals a debt of gratitude, as many of their stories point out to us.[*]

* Another kind of kazila, or taboo, is mentioned below (p. 122), namely, the prohibition to women to fish in the lake Mbosi or Mboasi, near Futilla.

The native herd in the white trader's employ talks to his sheep and goats as if they certainly understood him.

The plagues were sent by God (so the Hebrews say) to punish the oppressors of the children of Israel : so also any great scourge in this part of Africa is looked upon as a punishment. The locusts are at this moment eating up the Fjort's plantations here in Loango. The locusts are known by the name of Makonko, and are not entire strangers; but this year (1896-97) is the first time that the Fjort have seen them in such abundance. They do not know what to do to get rid of them; they say that their princes in the olden days would have done something and sent them away in a day.

A French official cut the long beard of poor old Maniprato, who was acting in the place of the King of Loango. The Fetish, who is the nephew of the great Mbunzi (S.W. wind), was very much annoyed at this action of the French official, and sent word to Mbunzi, and Mbunzi sent the plague of locusts, which in one night ate up the large banana plantation of the French mission. And now they are eating up the Fjort's plantations and his palm trees, and the poor Fjort has no longer any princes to send presents to Ngoio to calm the angry Mbunzi.

Bimbindi (pl. of Chimbindi), the spirits of the good who have departed this life, live in the woods, and are generally considered the enemies of mankind. But I knew a Chimbindi who was a very decent woman indeed. She was in love, and about to be married; but she fell sick, died, and was buried. Her lover was accused of having bewitched her, and he took casca and died. Her parents grieved greatly for her, for she was an only child. When she rose from the dead she found herself a slave, and married to a white man in Boma. She lived there with him until he went to Europe, when he freed her. She then tried to get back to her native town, which lay behind Malella. So she hired a canoe, and got the owners thereof to promise to paddle her there. But they took her to the south bank of the Congo, and sold her. Here she remained nearly three years, when she happened to meet some people of her own family, and they took her back to her parents. The parents were rejoiced to see her again; but they will not believe that she is a human being, and continue to treat her as the departed spirit of their daughter. I have tried to convince her that the Nganga Nkissi, or native doctor, must have played her some trick, and that she had been buried by him while in a trance, or while unconscious, and that he must have taken her to Boma and sold her there to his own profit; but she would not believe it.

But Bimbindi as a rule are hostile to the human race, and consequently greatly feared.

A certain chief owned a large town, and all the inhabitants were either his children or his relations. He was sorely troubled at times how to provide them all with animal food; and so he used to go into the woods, and set traps. One night he got up, and went to see if there was anything in his traps; and sure enough there was a large antelope in one of the traps. He made short work of its life by drawing his long knife and cutting its throat. Then he carried it home, and called upon all to get up and eat. They rejoiced greatly, and got up quickly enough to skin and cut up the antelope. It was then fairly divided, and each took away his share. And they all ate their shares, except the father, who put his away. Before the first cock crew, he got up again to look at his traps. Yes, there was another antelope. He killed and took it to his town, and again

roused the people up. They came, and again each took his
share. And they all ate their shares, except the father, who
put his share in the same place where he had kept his first share.
He now slept until sun-rise. About midday his son came to
him and said: " Father, I am hungry. Give me the antelope
you have kept in your shimbee (hut)." "No," he answered,
" I wish to sell that meat for cloth, even if I only get a fathom
or two for it." But the son pestered and bothered his father
until he waxed wroth and shot him dead. Then the father
called his people again, and said : " See, here is more meat for
you, take it and eat it." " Nay," they all said, " we cannot
eat this ; for your son was one of us ; he is of our family. But
we will cut him up, and give the meat to the princes round
about." And the princes were thankful for the meat, and gave
the bearers presents.

The next evening the father again went to visit his traps,
and thought he saw a huge something in one of them. He
ran up to the thing and tried to kill it ; but as he neared the
trap, the monster's arms embraced him and held him fast.
" Ah, ha ! " said the Chimbindi, " so you have dared to set
your traps in my woods, and to kill my antelopes. You shall
die." With this the Chimbindi cut the father's head off, and
hung his body to a tree by its feet. Now when his wife had
cooked his food, she called for him to come and eat. Receiving
no answer, she set out to look for him. " Surely he has gone
to look at his traps," she thought. So she went into the woods;
and after a little while she caught sight of the body hanging by
its legs to the tree. The head was not there; the Chimbindi
had taken it away with him. She examined the body carefully,
and at last convinced herself that it was that of her husband.

She sat down and wept. Then she got up, and went crying into the town. The people asked her what she was crying for, and she answered: " My husband has been killed, and I have seen his body in the woods." Then they tried to comfort her, telling her that she was mistaken. But she continued weeping, and offered to lead them to the place where he was hung. Then the whole tribe went with her ; and when they saw with their own eyes that their father was dead, they were sorely troubled and lamented. Then the Chimbindi returned, and utterly annihilated the tribe, cutting off their heads, and leaving their bodies as food for the eagles, and the crows, and the beasts of the woods that eat the flesh of men. So are those punished who kill a relation and offer his meat to be eaten.

But the natives have a weapon with which they can put the Chimbindi to flight, as we learn from the following story.

All preparations for a long stay out of town were made by a married couple, the parents of a little boy some four years old. As they could not take their little one with them on this occasion, they left sufficient food for him with a neighbour, and asked her to take care of him.   Soon the little boy felt hungry, and ran to the neighbour's house and asked her for food.   " What food, my child ? " she asked.   " But mother told me to come and ask you for food whenever I felt hungry."   " Your mother left no food with me, so that I cannot give you any ; and you can run away and play."   Each day the little boy went to the woman and asked her for food.   But each day she refused to give him any. So on the sixth day the little boy sat down and cried, saying : " Six days have passed and I have had no food.   I know not whither my parents have gone.   I shall surely die.   I will find them, I will go from here at once."   Then he got up and walked and walked all day, but could not find his parents. When the night came, he climbed up a big tree and sat in it and cried. And a Chimbindi came and found the boy. He called his friends together, and they asked: " Who is this ? " The little boy was very much afraid ; but he sang in a piteous voice : " My father and mother left me, they gave another food for me; but she did not give it to me ; and now I have come here to die." The Bimbindi came near to him and meant to kill him. When the little boy saw what the Bimbindi were about he cried bitterly for his mother.

Meanwhile the parents returned. The mother said : " Father, our little one has left our town, and has wandered away. Listen ! I hear him crying." " Nay," says the father, " we left food enough for him, why should he have left the town ? Look again for him." " No," says the mother ; " he is in the woods, and the Bimbindi will surely eat him, and we shall lose our little one." Then the father went to the market and bought some chili pepper, and loaded his gun with it. And the mother carried a calabash of pepper with her. " Let us go," said the father, " and search for him ! " And the mother soon found him, attracted by his cries. Then the father shot the Chimbindi just as he was climbing up the tree to kill his son. And the mother flew at the others that were looking on, and rubbed pepper into their eyes, so that they all ran away.

When the parents returned to the town they demanded an explanation from their neighbour ; but she could make no excuse for her conduct, so that the irate father shot the woman, saying : " You tried to kill my child, am I not right in killing you ? "

And the people said he was acting rightly.

Women have been captured by Bimbindi and made to live

with them, according to their tales, but have managed to escape. The Bimbindi have followed them to their towns, and to get rid of them these women have thrown pepper into their eyes, and poured boiling water over them.

I have also heard of an opposite case, where a Chimbindi has come to a town and married a girl and tried to live with her, but he would run away at daybreak, and all night he was busy eating insects and lizards; so she left him. Native women dare not go out at night alone for fear of meeting them; and any wailing noise they hear during the night they immediately put down to the Bimbindi.

The word *witch*, in our sense, I think, would correspond rather with that of Nganga Nkissi, the man learned in the art of mystery. But whereas our witch combines the office of spell-binder with that of curer, the Nganga Nkissi acts as the curer only, and the power that he exercises is not supposed to be his, but rather that of the Nkissi, or, as you would call it, his fetish. The sufferer goes to him to find out why it is that he suffers, and who it is that is making him suffer, and he divines the cause or person if he can; and if he cannot, advises the sufferer to knock a nail into the Nkissi, or fetish, and ask it to kill the person who is causing him so much pain.

The causer of the pain or suffering is called by the Fjort a Ndotchi, which has rather the sense of poisoner, and then spell-binder, or evil-wisher, or hypnotiser. This last personage is usually called the witch, and the Nganga Nkissi, the witch-doctor, by Europeans. The Ndotchi, it is true, may have poisoned some of his people to get rid of them, but he will have done this very secretly. He is not at all likely to go about proclaiming the fact that he can cast spells upon people, raise storms, or hypnotise, as such a proclamation would mean certain death. I am, therefore, sceptical when I hear Europeans talking about African witches and witchcraft, unless indeed, you call a poisoner a witch. It is the knowledge of poisons in the native, his horror of death, and his disbelief in death from natural causes, that force him to believe, when a death does take place, that poison has in all probability caused it. Accordingly, a so-called Ndotchi, or poisoner, is called upon to prove his innocence by being forced to undergo the ordeal by poison; he is made to eat two or three spoonfuls of the powdered bark of the " casca " tree, and drink a bottle of water. If he vomits, he is innocent; if the casca acts as a purge he is guilty, and at once slain. A native goes to sleep and dreams some fearful dream, awakes and feels himself spellbound. Up he gets and fires off a gun to frighten away the evil spirits. He imagines that he has an enemy who is seeking to kill him, and accuses people right and left of attempting to poison him, and gives them casca.

There are certain of the Ngangas who profess to work miracles like the magicians of old.

Women give their husbands certain medicines to cause them to love them, and try their own love for them, by undergoing different ordeals. For instance, a woman will bet another woman that she loves her husband more than she does. They will heat an iron and place it on their arms; if a blister is raised, they consider their great love as proved.

As you enter a village by some road or other you will often find the grass tied into a knot (*nteuo*) with medicines enclosed, to

prevent anyone bent on evil from passing that way ; or an arch*
formed by a string of feathers and charms, stretched across the
road from one pole to another, will keep away evil winds and
spirits.

Then, every town has some Nkissi or other to guard it.   One
will often notice an earthenware pot (*nduda*) half-full of sand,
containing two eggs, placed upon a stand.   It is said that these
eggs will explode with a fearful report, if anyone bent on evil
enters the town.

The Fjort have no legends about the creation, except such
as are easily traceable to the teachings of the missionaries of old,
settled in this country some 400 years ago.   Nzambi Mpungu
made the earth, or gave birth to Nzambi; and she brought forth
many children.   We are told nothing more about the creation.
The difference in colour between the black and white man is
accounted for by stories of the short-sightedness of the black
man.   The best, perhaps, is that given on a later page.

Then, we have tales which begin : " A long, long time ago,
before even our ancestors knew the use of fire, when they ate
grass like the animals," etc., which then go on to tell how a
river-spirit first pointed out to them the mandioca root and
the banana.   These I think go a long way to prove that the
agricultural age was prior to the pastoral and hunting age.
This river-spirit taught them the use of fire, and then came
the blacksmith, Mfuzi, (Loango, *Funzi*) and the iron and
copper age.

I do not think the people north of the Congo can yet be said to

---

* An ordinary knot in the grass means that some lady has marked the
place for a plantation, or that a passer-by has hidden something within a
certain distance from that knot.

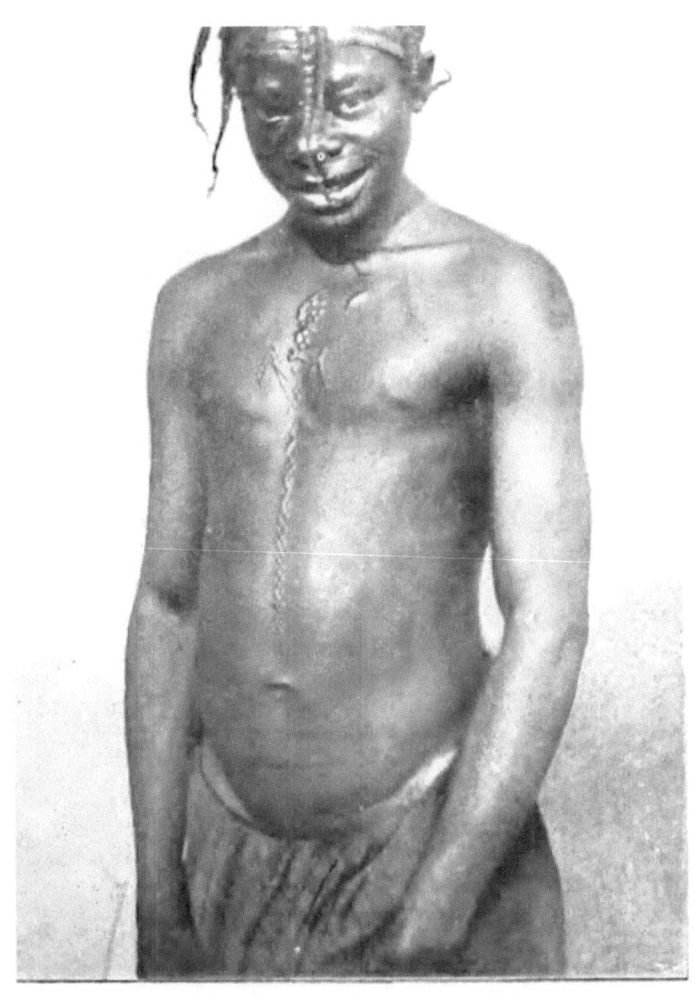

A BAKUTU WHO CAME TO LOANGO TO SEE NZAMBI.

To face page 18.

be in the Pastoral Age,* or to have passed through it, for, although they do keep a few goats, and fowls, and sheep, their attention is given more to the planting of mandioca, bananas, and potatoes than to the care of animals. But they certainly are hunters. They are also manufacturers of native grass-cloth, of knives, arms, and ornaments of iron and copper, and of ornaments made from European silver coins. They gather cotton, and spin a coarse kind of thread, with which they make *chinkutu*, arm-bags, and netted capes for their princes. They make beautiful caps from the fibre of the pine-apple, and mats from the leaves of the fubu-tree. And all these goods they dye red, black and yellow. Earthenware pots, vases, carafes, moringos, and pipes they make from the black clay that abounds in the different valleys. The fishermen make their own nets from the fibre of different trees, and floats from the bark of the baobab-tree.

Others gather the palm-nuts from the palm-trees, and extract the oil from them, dry them and crack them, and then sell the kernels and the oil to the European. Some go into the woods and collect the milky juice of several vines and trees, and sell it as caoutchouc, or rubber, to the white man.

And the women, as they hoe their fields, at times dig up pieces of preserved lightning (*aulo*, or *buangu*, gum copal), which they and their husbands also sell to the trader.

People collect round the shimbec, or hut, in which a woman

* There is no word in the KaCongo dialect to express the word shepherd. The nearest they have is *i lungo mbizi*, he who keeps animals ; but *mbizi* is used in the sense of wild animals. Thus a native missionary, or priest, in preaching in native-mouth to the children at the mission here in Loango talked of the shepherds who came to visit the child Christ and his Mother as the *galigneru*, from the Portuguese *gallinheiro*, one who looks after the fowls.

lies, about to give birth to a child, and fire off guns and shout to her to help her to bring it forth. The woman is attended by her mother, or other female relation; and the child is washed, sometimes in palm-wine, by them. As soon as the after-birth comes away, the woman walks away to the place where she is to take her hot bath. The women then throw the very hot water upon her parts with their hands.

Charm upon charm is attached to the infant; and the mother suckles it until it is nearly two years old, being separated from her husband until she has weaned the child.

When a boy arrives at the age of puberty he is circumcised, and if he is wealthy a dance is given in his honour. A girl arriving at the same age is closely watched. The moment of her first menstruation is marked by the firing off of a gun, and this is followed by a dance. And now, while she little suspects it, she is caught and forced into what the natives call the paint-house. Here she is painted red, and carefully fed and treated, until they consider her ready for marriage, when she is washed and led to her husband. But if she has not a husband waiting for her, she is covered over with a red cloth, or handkerchief, and taken round by women to the different towns, until someone is found anxious to have her.

Should a man wish to marry a girl, he has to present her parents with goods according to the value placed upon her by them. In fixing the value, her position and wealth have to be considered. He can marry her according to different rites, such as those of Lembe or Funzi. On such occasions a certain kind of native-made copper bracelet is given to her by the husband, and worn also by him. She swears to be faithful to him, and to die and be buried with him. Formerly these wives were

buried alive with their husbands, but the custom is now dying
out.

Or a man may not have money enough to marry. So he pro-
poses to give the girl so much of his earnings if she will live
with him. He presents the parents with some small donation,
and they live together until he can marry her.

But virgins may be used by a man for a certain payment,
and afterwards put aside. These women are then at the service
of anyone who chooses to pay them. This life is not looked
upon as being immoral by them, and in no way stands in the
way of future marriage. And it is a strange fact that these
women do not seem to lose their sense of modesty. They seem
to think that it is natural that their desires should be satisfied,
and that until they are married they are in their right to live in
this way.

A man may marry as many wives as he has wealth enough
to obtain; and as they all make their plantations he is not likely
to starve so long as he treats them properly. But the wives
quarrel for his favours, and so very often a very-much-married
man does not live so happily as one who has (say) two wives.

When the bridegroom takes his bride from the paint-house,
he is generally supposed to give a dance, and this dance is kept up
all night round about his house.

Unfaithfulness in a princess used not very long ago to be
punished by burying her into the ground up to her neck,
leaving only her head visible, and then leaving her to starve
and die. The adulterer used to be impaled and allowed to rot.

If a KaCongo princess, one of the wives of KaCongo, was
found to have crossed the River Loango Luz, a certain prince
called Maloango had the right to break off her ivory bracelet

and declare her a whore. The same law applied to any of the
wives of Loango who crossed over into KaCongo.

" I am in debt " is the cry of nearly every native one meets;
and thus he stirs himself to action. He now owes the Nganga
Nkissi for some charms, or the Nganga bilongo, for some
medicine, or else he has borrowed goods to help him to bury
some relation. Wealthy men lend people goods, such as a hoe
to a woman to bury her child. In her grief she perhaps might
bury it with the body. Then the wealthy man would ask her
for his hoe and she would have to dig it up again. The man
would say to her: " This hoe smells of death; keep it and pay
me for it." The woman having nothing to pay him with, the
wealthy man would take one of her little daughters to live with
his wives. The woman might repay him at any time up to the
time when the girl should come to the age of puberty; but once
he put the girl into the paint-house she became his " daughter
of the cloth," a household slave. Men wanting money used
to go to these men and accept loans, thus becoming their
dependants.

The burden of debt seems to have been the only great motive
power in the life of the Fjort. Thus all along the coast you will
find that the traders have always been forced to lend money, or
rather goods, to native princes and traders, and then use all
their knowledge of native law to oblige them to give them the
produce promised in exchange.

When a child dies it is marked round the eyes and about the
body with white and red chalk, and is buried perhaps the next
day. The slave, or poor man, is also buried quickly without
any particular ceremony. The rich man (or woman) when
dead, is smoked dry over a smoky fire wrapped up in endless

lengths of cloth according to his wealth, and after some months
is buried in an imposing case very similar to that of a prince.

A prince dies. Immediately it is known, all other princes
either go themselves with, or else send, their people dressed in
feathers, with drums and bugles, to cry. These visitors receive
unlimited drink, and dance and sing until they are tired, and
then they return to their towns. The Nganga Nkissi is set to
work to find out who it is that has caused the death of the
prince; and many people are forced to take casca. Many
deaths, therefore, follow that of the prince.

His body is smoked and watched by his wives in the back
room (as it were), while in the front half of the shimbec the
prince's wealth, in the shape of ewers, basins, figure ornaments,
pots, pipes, glassware, etc., is on view. One of his wives will
generally be found walking about in front of the shimbec, throwing her arms about and crying. This may last for a year or
more before the body is buried.

The coffin is a case, perhaps 15 feet long, 4 feet broad, 6 feet
high, covered over with red save-list. White braid is nailed by
means of brass-headed chair-nails in diamond-shaped designs, all
over the red cloth. The coffin (into which the dried body,
wrapped in cloth is placed) is then put on the funeral car. Stuffed
tigers, an umbrella, and other ornaments are placed upon the
top of the coffin. The whole is then drawn to the burial ground
by hundreds of assembled guests, who sing and dance by the
way.

The grave is ready; and the coffin is lowered into it. Then
one or two of his wives (10 years ago) jumped in, or (as is the
case to this day, a little north of Loango) two small boys are
placed in the grave beside the coffin; and all are buried. His

relations proclaim the new prince, and place over his shoulder a wreath of grass. The people then return to the prince's town and dance.

A year or two after this, a kind of festival in honour of the departed is kept. An effigy in straw of the late prince is placed in a shimbec, seated behind a table which bears such earthenware, glassware, and ornaments as belonged to him, and were not placed over his grave when he was buried. The rest of his wives, who from the time of his death until that of his burial have never washed themselves, have now only certain marks in charcoal upon their faces, and walk about the place more reasonably. Some of his children take it in turns to beat a drum and sing near to the shimbec. Visitors, bringing their offerings, come and congratulate the new prince upon what we should call his coronation; and he receives them sitting perhaps under the shade of some great tree. The relics of the late prince are visited; and then dancing, and singing, and eating, and drinking commence; and this is continued for perhaps three or four days.

II.

HOW A NATIVE STORY IS TOLD.

PERHAPS it may interest you to know how a story is told.

Imagine, then, a village in a grove of graceful palm trees. The full moon is shining brightly upon a small crowd of Negroes seated round a fire in an open space in the centre of the village. One of them has just told a story, and his delighted audience demands another. Thus he begins :

" Let us tell another story ; let us be off ! "

All then shout : " Pull away ! "

" Let us be off ! " he repeats.

And they answer again : " Pull away ! "

Then the story teller commences :

" There were two brothers, the Smart Man and the Fool. And it was their habit to go out shooting to keep their parents supplied with food. Thus one day they went together into the mangrove swamp, just as the tide was going down, to watch for the fish as they nibbled at the roots of the trees. The Fool saw a fish, fired at it and killed it. The Smart Man fired also, but at nothing, and then ran up to the Fool and said : ' Fool, have you killed anything ? '

" ' Yes, Smart Man, I am a fool ; but I killed a fish.'

" ' Indeed, you are a fool,' answered the Smart Man, ' for when I fired I hit the fish that went your way ; so that the fish you think you killed is mine. Here, give it to me.'

" The Fool gave the Smart Man the fish. Then they went to their town, and the Smart Man, addressing his father, said: ' Father, here is a fish that your son shot, but the Fool got nothing.' "

Here the crowd join in, and sing over the last sentence two or three times.

Then the narrator continues :

" The mother prepared and cooked the fish, and the father and the Smart Man ate it, giving none to the Fool.

" Then they went again ; and the Fool fired, and with his first shot killed a big fish.

" ' Did you hear me fire ? " says the Smart Man.

" ' No,' answers the Fool.

" ' No?' returned the Smart Man; ' see then the fish I killed.'

" ' All right,' says the Fool, ' take the fish.'

" When they got home they gave the fish to their mother ; and when she had cooked it, the Smart Man and his father ate it, but gave none to the Fool. But as they were enjoying the fish, a bone stuck in the father's throat. Then the Smart Man called to the Fool and bade him go for a doctor.

" ' No,' says the Fool, ' I cannot. I felt that something would happen.' And he sings :

> ' Every day you eat my fish, you call me Fool,
>   And would let me starve.' "

The crowd here join in, and sing the Fool's song over and over again.

" ' How can you sing,' says the Smart Man, ' when you see that our father is suffering ?

" But the Fool goes on singing :

> ' You eat and eat unto repletion ;
> A bone sticks in your throat ;
> And now your life is near completion,
> The bone is still within your throat.

> ' So you, smart brother, killed the fish,
> And gave the fool to eat ?
> Nay ! but now he's dead perhaps you wish
> You'd given the fool to eat.' "

The crowd go on singing this until they are tired ; and the story-teller continues :

" While yet the Fool was singing, the father died. Then the neighbours came and joined the family circle, and asked the Fool how it was that he could go on singing now that his father was dead.

" And the Fool answered them, saying : ' Our Father made us both, one a smart man, the other a fool. The Fool kills the food, and they eat it, giving none to the Fool. They must not blame him, therefore, if he sings while they suffer. He suffered hunger while they had plenty.

" And when the people had considered the matter, they gave judgement in favour of the Fool, and departed.

"The father had died, and so had been justly punished for not having given the Fool food.

" He who eats fish with much oil must suffer from indigestion.

" And now I have finished my story."

All answer, " Just so ! "

" To-morrow may you chop palm-kernels," says the narrator, as he gets up and walks away.

A lady telling a story begins by shouting out the words: "Viado! Nkia? (An antelope! How big?)"

The crowd answer: "Nzoka (two fathoms)."

Then the narrator begins:

"Once there was a man who had a wife, but he fell in love with another woman. His wife was heavy with child, but he neglected her. He used to go out fishing; but instead of giving his wife the fish, he gave it to his lover. When he shot an antelope he gave his wife none of it. If he trapped a bird it went to the wicked woman."

The narrator sings:

> "The poor starved wife
> Brought forth a son,
> She gave it life,
> Poor weakly one!"

Then all join in this song in tones of disgust.

"The son grew up and complained to his mother that while he had eaten of the produce of her farm he had not yet eaten any food killed by his father, nor even worn a cloth given by him.

"One day a friend gave him a knife, and he immediately, unknown to his mother, went to the woods and hills to cut some muchinga, or native string. He tried to kill some game by throwing his knife at it, but to no purpose. So before he left for home he set a trap to catch some bird or other. He grieved at his bad luck.

"Next morning he went out again, and to his intense relief found a guinea-fowl in his trap. He ran away home with his prize, and, while yet afar off, shouted to his mother:

" ' Mother, get the fundi (tapioca) ready ! '

" Fundi ! my son. How is this ? You return too early for meal-time and call for fundi. Your father has taken no notice of me and has brought me no food : whence then, my son, hast thou got food for me to cook ? '

" ' Never you mind, mother, get the fundi ready.'

" The mother prepared the fundi, and the son laid the bird at her feet. When she saw that her son could bring her food, she no longer thought of her troubles or her husband. When the food was ready, the mother called her son and named him Zingu (to continue to live), for now they could eat and live without the help of a father.

" About this time the husband had grown tired of his concubine and sent her away, so that having no one to cook for him, he remained in his shimbee (house) hungering.

" When he heard that his son now went out hunting, and had plenty of food, he sneaked out of his shimbee and clapped his hands and begged his son to give him food.

" He sang :

> ' My son, can it be true
> That you me food deny ?
> Upon my knees I sue,
> My son, let me not die.' "

All present repeat this song plaintively.

" Then the mother replied :

> ' You first denied us food ;
> We starved and nearly died ;
> We will not give him food
> Who kept that girl supplied.'

" Another day, when the son had been lucky and caught a
bird, after killing and cleaning it, he said :   ' Mother, time was
when we nearly died of hunger, but now we have plenty ; and
now that I am a man you shall need neither cloth nor food.'

" And as they were feeding, the father. very thin and weak,
crawled out of his shimbec, and cried :

> ' Oh, Zinga, my son, Zinga,
> Will you let your father die ?
> Oh, Kengi, my wife, Kengi,
> Here starving do I lie.' "

All around sing this song in a supplicating tone.

" When the son heard his father crying so bitterly, he was
greatly moved, and prayed his mother to put some food upon a
plate and send it to him ; but the mother refused, saying that
he deserved none.

" Then the son wept and sang:

> ' Mother, father wronged us
> When he starved us ;
> Let us feed him now he asks us,
> Or God may kill us.'

" And then he put some food upon a plate and was about to
give it to his father, when his father dropped down dead from
starvation.

" An enquiry was held to find out how the father had come
to die ; and when the people had heard all they gave judgement.

" He did not give his wife and child food when they needed
it.   They were in their right when they gave him none when
he asked for it.   He died by the avenging hand of the Great
Spirit."

I will conclude this chapter with a native tale of a practical joker, a character who is as much *en evidence* in Africa, I regret to say, as he is in other parts of the world.

There were two men who from their childhood had been fast friends, and never were known to have quarrelled with one another. So great was their friendship that they had made their farms close to one another. They were divided one from the other only by a native path.

Now there was a wicked wit in their town, who had determined, if possible, to make these chums quarrel. This man made a coat, one side or half of which was red in colour, while the other was blue. And he walked past these two chums as they were busy on their farms, making enough noise to attract their attention. Each of the chums looked up to see who it was that was passing, and then went on with his work.

" Ugh, say ! did you see that man ? " said one.

" Yes," answered the other.

" Did you notice the bright coat he wore ? "

" Yes."

" What colour should you say it was ? "

" Why, blue, of course."

" Blue, man ! why, it was a kind of red ! "

" Nay, friend, I am sure it was blue."

" Nonsense ! I know it was red, but——"

" Well ! you are a fool ! "

" A fool, how now ! we have been friends all our lives, and now you call me a fool ! let us fight ; our friendship is at an end." And the quondam chums fought.

Then their women screamed and interfered, and managed to separate them.

Then the wit walked quietly back, and saw the two chums seated each in his own farm, with his elbows resting on his knees and his head between his hands.

Then they saw through the joke and they were sorry ; and they ordered the wit never to come that way again.

But the women cursed the wit and hoped that he would soon die.

III.

HOW THE WIVES RESTORED THEIR HUSBAND TO LIFE.

A CERTAIN man, named Nenpetro, had three wives, Ndoza'ntu (the Dreamer), Songa'nzila (the Guide), and Fulla Fulla (the Raiser of the Dead). Now Nenpetro was a great hunter; and one day he killed an antelope, and gave it to his three wives. They ate it, and after a time complained of hunger. Nenpetro went out shooting again, and killed a monkey. They ate this also, but still complained of hunger. "Oh," says Nenpetro, "nothing but an ox will satisfy you people." So off he went on the track of an ox. He followed the tracks for a long way, and at last caught sight of it as it was feeding with two or three others. He stalked it carefully, and shot it; but before he could reload, another angry ox charged him, and killed him.

Now in town they knew nothing of all this; but his wives grew very hungry, and cried for him to come back to them. Still he returned not. Then Ndoza'ntu dreamt that he had been killed by an ox, but that he had killed an ox before he fell.

"Come along," said Songa'nzila; "I will show you the road."

Thus they set out, and marched up hill and down dale, through woods and across rivers, until towards nightfall they came up to

D

the place where their husband lay dead. And now **Fulla Fulla** went into the woods and collected herbs and plants, and set about raising him from the dead.

Then the three women began to quarrel and wonder into whos shimbec Nenpetro would first enter.

" I dreamt that he was dead," said Ndoza'ntu.

" But I showed you where he lay dead," said Songa'nzila.

" And I have brought him back to life," said Fulla Fulla, as the husband gradually gave signs of life.

" Well ! let us each cook a pot of food, and take it to him as soon as he can eat ; and let him decide out of which pot he will take his first meal."

So two killed fowls, and cooked them each in her own pot, while the third cooked some pig in hers. And Nenpetro took the pot of pig that Fulla Fulla had cooked, and said : " When you dreamt that I was dead, you did not give me food, Ndoza'ntu ; for I was not yet found. And when you, Songa'nzila, had shown the others the road, I was still unfit to eat ; but when Fulla Fulla gave me back my life, then was I able to eat the pig she gave me. The gift therefore of Fulla Fulla is the most to be prized."

And the majority of the people said he was right in his judgement ; but the women round about said he should have put the food out of the three pots into one pot, and have eaten the food thus mixed.

IV.

HOW NSASSI* (GAZELLE) GOT MARRIED.

NENPETRO had two wives, and they each gave birth to a beautiful daughter. As they were a rich family, they determined not to take a present for their daughters on being asked in marriage, but to give them to him who could find out their names. They called one Lunga and the other Lenga.

The daughters grew up as beautiful as their parents could have wished, and were now of a marriageable age. The antelope then came to the parents, and, placing his large bundle of cloth and valuables at their feet, asked them to give him their daughters in marriage.

" We cannot accept your generous presents, for we have sworn to give our daughters only to the man who can guess their names."

The antelope scampered off and wondered how he could possibly find out their names.

Then Nsassi, a well-known prince of a town some way off, came along followed by his faithful dog, and asked Nenpetro for his daughters.

" Nay, guess their names, my son, and thou shalt have them."

* So in the Musurongo dialect. In the Cabenda and Loango dialects the word is Nsessi.

" Well! what do you call them ? "

" No, I may not tell you."

And the dog sat watching his master and heard all that was said, and felt for him. Nsassi went away sore-hearted; for the daughters of Nenpetro were beautiful to behold, and he yearned for them. So grieved was he, that he did not miss his dog, but marched straight back to his town to devise some means by which he might find out their names.

And now Nenpetro called his daughters to him by their names, " Lunga! Lenga! come here."

And the dog heard their names and said: " Oh I must run off and tell my father the names of these beautiful daughters, that he may marry them and be happy."

And off he trotted along the road, until he was nearly dead with hunger. Then he looked about for something to eat, and after some trouble caught a wild kitten. When he had eaten it, he set off again full of happiness, until he began to think over in his mind the names of Nenpetro's daughters. Alas! he had forgotten them. What was he to do? He resolved to go back again to Nenpetro's town. After a weary journey, he arrived there about midnight, and then slept until well into the next day.

" Oh! Lunga and Lenga, give that little dog of Nsassi's some food."

The daughters gave him food, but no water to drink; but he licked their hands and thanked them. Off he set again as happy as possible, full of the importance of his mission. He met a clear stream of water, and so overcome was he by thirst, that he forgot his errand and drank deeply of the waters. When he had satisfied himself, he tried to think of the names of Nenpetro's daughters, but he could not. So he had to return again to Nenpetro's town and sleep there that night.

The next morning Nenpetro called Lunga and Lenga, and said: " My children, give food and drink to Nsassi's dog."

And the daughters gave him both food and drink. And he was satisfied, and once more set off towards Nsassi's town. He arrived there safely this time, having thought of nothing else but the names of Nenpetro's daughters and his father's happiness along the road.

And Nsassi, when he saw him, was glad, and called him, and said: " O, my dear dog, where hast thou been ? and canst thou tell me the names of Nenpetro's daughters ? "

And the dog answered: " Yes, my master, I know their names."

" Tell me, then."

" First, thou must pay me, father."

Nsassi killed a pig and gave it to his dog. Then the dog told him the names of the beautiful girls, and all that had happened. And Nsassi was delighted, and gave a great dance ; and all in town were happy, as now it was certain that Nsassi would get the daughters of Nenpetro in marriage.

Then Nsassi and his dog set out to claim the daughters of Nenpetro. But the dancing and singing had made them very thirsty, so that when they came to the clear water they drank deeply. And when they were satisfied they found to their dismay that they had forgotten the names of the girls.

Then the dog went alone to Nenpetro's town, and again heard the father call his daughters by their names. They gave him food and drink, and he immediately returned .to his master. Then they neither ate nor drank on the road, but went straight

for Nenpetro's town.   And Nsassi called the daughters of
Nenpetro by their names and claimed them as his wives.

And Nenpetro said, "Take them, my son, for thou hast
fulfilled the condition upon which I promised them."

And the antelope declared war against Nsassi, and they
fought; but Nsassi gained the victory, and killed the antelope
and ate him.

V

THE VANISHING WIFE.

Two brothers lived in a certain town. They were called Buite and Swarmi.

Swarmi was married and had servants to wait upon him; but Buite was alone and despised. As Buite had no one to cook for him, he used to eat palm-kernels, which he daily brought in from the bush.

Swarmi treated Buite very badly, never asking him to join him at his meals, or enter in any way into the festivities of his family; so that Buite determined to leave his town, and live alone far away in the bush. So one day, without saying anything, he left his brother, and walked, and walked, and walked, until at nightfall he arrived at a deep valley, fertile and thickly planted with palm-trees. Far away at the bottom of this damp valley, beneath the shade of the high trees, palms and rushes, Buite built himself a little shed—a roof, supported upon sticks, about a foot in height above the ground. In this damp hovel he spread out his mat to sleep upon, and lighted his fire to cook his solitary meals.

Tired and weary of life, Buite one night fell asleep, and dreamt that a beautiful girl called him, that he rose and followed her, and that she led him through the thick jungle and woods, until they arrived at a river. Here she told him to tap on the ground

three times ; and to his surprise a canoe appeared.   He tapped
the canoe three times, and paddles made their appearance. Then
she told him to go and fish, and bring her food, that she might
cook it for him ; but that he should cut the heads off the fish,
as she could not bear to see them.   And he dreamt that he did
so, and returned to find the girl waiting for him to cook the fish.
Then he awoke, and could sleep no longer that night.

The next morning he got up and, remembering his dream,
travelled through the jungle and woods, until he came to the
river he had seen in his dream. And he tapped the ground, and
lo ! there appeared the canoe.   He tapped the canoe, and there
were the paddles.   Then he went and fished, and cut the heads
off the fish, and returned to his wretched hovel.   But the shed
had disappeared, and in its place was a large house, beautifully
furnished, and all the necessary out-houses, and above everything, the beautiful girl, who came forward to meet him, just as
if she had been accustomed to do so every day, and she also had
nine little servants to wait upon her.   And when she told him,
that she had come to comfort him, he was very pleased and
loved her very much.

And every day, when he went out fishing, she would send one
of the little ones with him, to carry the fish.   And people who
passed that way were astonished at the liberal treatment bestowed
upon them by Buite, and wondered where he had got his wife
and riches from.   His brother, Swarmi, would not believe in
Buite's prosperity, and determined to visit him.

Now Buite each day went fishing, taking one of his wife's
boys with him.   But after a time he got tired of always cutting
off the fishes' heads.

And it so happened one day that he did not cut off the heads of the fish. When the boy saw this, he cried out and protested, saying that his mother did not like to see a fish's head.

But Buite asked him if it was for him, a servant, to talk in that way to his master. And the boy left for the house, carrying the fish with him. But after a time Buite ran after the boy, and caught him up just before he got home, and cut the heads of the fish off, so that his wife should not see them.

And this happened eight times with eight different servants of his wife. Each time the boy protested; each time Buite scolded him, and then, repenting, ran after the boy and cut the heads of the fish off.

The ninth time he took the youngest boy, Parrot by name, and fished, and gave the entire fish to him to carry home. And Parrot cried very much and protested, but was frightened by Buite's imperious manner, and ran away home with the fish. And Buite ran after him, and ran, and ran, and ran, but could not catch Parrot up.

And Parrot arrived, and showed the fish to the woman; and immediately the house vanished; and the out-houses, and the servants, and beautiful furniture, and lastly the lovely wife, all disappeared, so that when Buite arrived, all out of breath, he no longer saw his house, or wife, or servants, but only his brother, Swarmi, who just then turned up to visit him.

And Buite was very sorry, and wept very much; and Swarmi more than ever despised him, and left him once more alone.

VI

ANOTHER VANISHING WIFE.

THERE were two sons of one mother, one named Mavungu, and the other Luemba. Luemba was a fine child, and grew up to be a handsome man. Mavungu was puny and miserable-looking, and as he came to man's estate became dwarfish and mean-looking. The mother always treated Luemba very well: but she maltreated Mavungu, and made him sleep outside the house beneath the mango-trees; and often when he approached her, to beg for food, she would throw the water she had cooked the beans in over his head.

Mavungu could not stand this bad treatment any longer; so he ran away into the woods, and wandered far away from home, until he came to a river. Here he discovered a canoe, and so determined to use it as a means of carrying him still further from his town. And he paddled and paddled, until he came to a huge tree, that overspread the river and prevented him from paddling. So he laid his paddle down, and caught hold of the leaves of the fuba-tree to pull his canoe along. But no sooner had he begun to pull the leaves of the fuba-tree, than he heard a voice, as if of a woman, faintly crying: "You are hurting me! please take care."

Mavungu wondered, but still pulled himself along.

" Take care! you are breaking my legs off," said the voice.

Still Mavungu pulled until a leaf broke off and instantly became changed into a beautiful woman. This startled Mavungu, so that he pulled many other leaves off the fuba-tree. Each leaf turned into a man, or a woman ; his canoe was so full that he could not pull it any longer.

Then the first woman told him that she had come to be his wife, and comfort him; and Mavungu was no longer afraid, but was very happy. Then the wife appealed to her fetish, and said: " Am I to marry a man so deformed as this one is ? " And immediately Mavungu became changed into a beautifully-formed man.

" Is he to be dressed like that?" she cried; and straightway his dress was changed.

In the same magical way did the wife build Mavungu a large house and town for his people, so that he wanted nothing that was needful to a powerful prince. And as people passed that way they were astonished at the transformation, and wondered where Mavungu had obtained his beautiful wife. And his mother and brother and whole family came to see him; and he treated them liberally and sent them away loaded with presents. But, having been expressly warned by his wife to say nothing to them as to the origin of his happiness, he left them in ignorance of that fact.

Then his people invited Mavungu to their town, but his wife advised him not to go, and so he stayed at home. But after having received many invitations he finally agreed, in spite of his wife's advice, to visit them. He promised, however, not to eat any of the food given to him. When he arrived in town his mother placed poisoned food before him and urged him

to partake thereof, but he refused. And then they asked about his beautiful wife, and being taken off his guard, he replied:
" Oh, when I left you I wandered through the woods."

But when he had got thus far he heard his wife's voice ringing through the woods:

" Oh! Ma-vu-ng-u-a-a-a!" and immediately he remembered, and got up and ran away home.

His wife was very cross with him, and told him plainly that she would not help him the next time he made a fool of himself.

Some time after this Mavungu again went to visit his family. His wife said nothing, neither asking him to stay at home, nor giving him her consent to his going. When he had greeted his mother and had partaken of food, the family again asked him to tell them from whence he had obtained his wife.

And he said: " When I left you, owing to your bad treatment, I wandered through the woods and came to a river. Dear me! where has my beautiful hat gone?"

" Your brother has taken it, to put it in the sun," said the mother, " but continue."

" I found a canoe with a paddle in it. Where has my coat gone?"

" Your brother has taken that also."

" And I paddled and paddled. Why have you taken my beautiful cloth?"

" To have it washed, of course."

" I paddled until I came to a big tree. Nay, why not leave me my shirt? and as I pulled off the leaves of the fuba-tree, they turned into my wife and her attendants. But I am naked!"

Then Mavungu remembered, and ran away to his town, only to find that it and his beautiful wife had disappeared. And when the people heard the whole story, they said it served Mavungu right for being so foolish as to want to please his people, who had been his enemies all along, rather than please his wife, who had been so good to him.

VII.

THE JEALOUS WIFE.

Two wives busied themselves preparing chicoanga, or native bread, for their husband, who purposed going into the bush for six months to trade. Each of these women had a child; and the husband, as he left them, adjured them to be very careful with the children, and see that no harm came to them. They promised faithfully to attend to his entreaty.

When it was nearly time for the husband to return, the women said : " Let us go and fish, that we may give our husband some good food when he returns."

But as they could not leave the children alone, one had to stay with them while the other fished. The elder wife went first, and stayed in the fishing-ground for two or three days to smoke what she had caught. Then the younger wife left to fish, and the elder remained to take care of the children.

Now the child of the younger wife was a much brighter and more intelligent child than that of the elder; and this made the latter jealous and angry. So she determined to murder the child, and get it out of the way while its mother was fishing. She sharpened a razor until it easily cut off the hairs on her arm, and then put it away until the evening when the children should be asleep. And when it was evening and they were fast asleep, she went to the place where the child was accustomed to sleep, and killed it. The other child awoke, and in its fright ran out of the house and took refuge with a neighbour.

In the morning the elder wife went to look at her evil work, thinking to put the child away before its mother should return. But when she looked again at the child she was horror-struck to find that she had killed her own child. She wept as she picked up its little body; and wrapping it up in her cloth she ran away with it into the woods, and disappeared.

The husband returned and at once missed his elder wife. He questioned the younger one; but she could only repeat to him what her child had told her, namely, that during the night the elder wife had killed her child. The husband would not believe this story, and asked his friends, the bushmen who had come with him, to help him to search for his wife. They agreed, and scoured the woods the whole day, but without success.

The next day one of the bushmen came across a woman who was nursing something; so he hid and listened to her singing. The poor woman was for ever shaking the child, saying:

" Are you always going to sleep like this? Why don't you awake? Why don't you talk? See! See! it is your mother that nurses you."

" Surely," said the bushman, " this must be my friend's wife. I will go to him and tell him that I have found her."

" Let us go," said the husband; and as they approach her they hide themselves so that she cannot see them. And they find her still shaking the child and still singing the same sad song.

Then the father calls in her relations, and together they go
to the woods, and make her prisoner. And when they saw that
the child had been really murdered, they gave casca to the
woman; and it killed her. Then they burnt her body, and
scattered its ashes to the wind.

VIII.

NGOMBA'S BALLOON.

FOUR little maidens one day started to go out fishing. One of them was suffering sadly from sores, which covered her from head to foot. Her name was Ngomba. The other three, after a little consultation, agreed that Ngomba should not accompany them ; and so they told her to go back.

"Nay," said Ngomba, "I will do no such thing. I mean to catch fish for mother as well as you."

Then the three maidens beat Ngomba until she was glad to run away. But she determined to catch fish also, so she walked and walked, she hardly knew whither, until at last she came upon a large lake. Here she commenced fishing and singing :

> "If my mother
>   [She catches a fish and puts it in her basket.]
> Had taken care of me,
>   [She catches another fish and puts it in her basket.]
> I should have been with them,
>   [She catches another fish and puts it in her basket.]
> And not here alone."
>   [She catches another fish and puts it in her basket.]

E

But a Mpunia (murderer) had been watching her for some time, and now he came up to her and accosted her: .

" What are you doing here ? "

" Fishing.   Please, don't kill me !   See, I am full of sores, but I can catch plenty of fish."

The Mpunia watched her as she fished and sang :

> " Oh, I shall surely die !
>> [She catches a fish and puts it in her basket.]
> Mother, you will never see me !
>> [She catches another fish and puts it in her basket.]
> But I don't care,
>> [She catches another fish and puts it in her basket.]
> For no one cares for me."
>> [She catches another fish and puts it in her basket.]

" Come with me," said the Mpunia.

" Nay, this fish is for mother, and I must take it to her."

" If you do not come with me, I will kill you."

> "Oh ! Am I to die
>> [She catches a fish and puts it in her basket.]
> On the top of my fish ?
>> [She catches another fish and puts it in her basket.]
> If mother had loved me,
>> [She catches another fish and puts it in her basket.]
> To live I should wish.
>> [She catches another fish and puts it in her basket.]

Take me and cure me, dear Mpunia, and I will serve you."

The Mpunia took her to his home in the woods, and cured her.   Then he placed her in the paint-house and married her.

Now the Mpunia was very fond of dancing, and Ngomba danced beautifully, so that he loved her very much, and made her mistress over all his prisoners and goods.

" When I go out for a walk," he said to her, " I will tie this string round my waist; and that you may know when I am still going away from you, or returning, the string will be stretched tight as I depart, and will hang loose as I return."

Ngomba pined for her mother, and therefore entered into a conspiracy with her people to escape. She sent them every day to cut the leaves of the mateva-palm, and ordered them to put them in the sun to dry. Then she set them to work to make a huge ntenda, or basket. And when the Mpunia returned, he remarked to her that the air was heavy with the smell of mateva.

Now she had made all her people put on clean clothes, and when they knew that he was returning, she ordered them to come to him and flatter him. So now they approached him, and some called him " father" and others " uncle "; and others told him how he was a father and a mother to them. And he was very pleased, and danced with them.

The next day when he returned he said he smelt mateva.

Then Ngomba cried, and told him that he was both father and mother to her, and that if he accused her of smelling of mateva, she would kill herself.

He could not stand this sadness, so he kissed her and danced with her until all was forgotten.

The next day Ngomba determined to try her ntenda, to see if it would float in the air. Thus four women lifted it on high, and gave it a start upwards, and it floated beautifully. Now the Mpunia happened to be up a tree, and he espied this great ntenda floating in the air; and he danced and sang for joy, and wished to call Ngomba, that she might dance with him.

That night he smelt mateva again, and his suspicions were

aroused; and when he thought how easily his wife might escape him, he determined to kill her. Accordingly, he gave her to drink some palm-wine that he had drugged. She drank it, and slept as he put his sommo (the iron that the natives make red hot, and with which they burn the hole through the stem of their pipes) into the fire. He meant to kill her by pushing this red hot wire up her nose.

But as he was almost ready, Ngomba's little sister, who had changed herself into a cricket and hidden herself under her bed, began to sing. The Mpunia heard her and felt forced to join in and dance, and thus he forgot to kill his wife. But after a time she ceased singing, and then he began to heat the wire again. The cricket then sang again, and again he danced and danced, and in his excitement tried to wake Ngomba to dance also. But she refused to awake, telling him that the medicine he had given her made her feel sleepy. Then he went out and got some palm-wine, and as he went she drowsily asked him if he had made the string fast. He called all his people, dressed himself, and made them all dance.

The cock crew.

The iron wire was still in the fire. The Mpunia made his wife get up and fetch more palm-wine.

Then the cock crew again, and it was daylight.

When the Mpunia had left her for the day, Ngomba determined to escape that very day. So she called her people and made them try the ntenda again; and when she was certain that it would float, she put all her people, and all the Mpunia's ornaments, into it. Then she got in and the ntenda began to float away over the tree-tops in the direction of her mother's town.

When the Mpunia, who was up a tree, saw it coming towards

him, he danced and sang for joy, and only wished that his wife had been there to see this huge ntenda flying through the air. It passed just over his head, and then he knew that the people in it were his. So that he ran after it in the tops of the trees, until he saw it drop in Ngomba's town. And he determined to go there also and claim his wife.

The ntenda floated round the house of Ngomba's mother, and astonished all the people there, and finally settled down in front of it. Ngomba cried to the people to come and let them out. But they were afraid and did not dare, so that she came out herself and presented herself to her mother.

Her relations at first did not recognise her; but after a little while they fell upon her and welcomed her as their long-lost Ngomba.

Then the Mpunia entered the town and claimed Ngomba as his wife.

"Yes," her relations said, "she is your wife, and you must be thanked for curing her of her sickness."

And while some of her relations were entertaining the Mpunia, others were preparing a place for him and his wife to be seated. They made a large fire, and boiled a great quantity of water, and dug a deep hole in the ground. This hole they covered over with sticks and a mat, and when all was ready they led the Mpunia and his wife to it, and requested them to be seated. Ngomba sat near her husband, who, as he sat down, fell into the hole. The relations then brought boiling water and fire, and threw it over him until he died.

THE WICKED HUSBAND.

" Cut you more palm-nuts? why, I am for ever cutting palm-nuts! What on earth do you do with them? I cut enough in one day to keep you for a week," said the husband to his wife.

" Nay," said the wife, " what am I to do? first, one of your relations comes to me, and asks me for a few, then another, and another, and so on, until they are all gone. Can I refuse to give them ? "

" Well, as you know, its a long way to where the palm-trees grow. If you want palm-nuts, you can come with me and carry them back with you."

" Nay, I cannot go so far, for I have just put the mandioca in the water."

" But you must go ! "

" Nay, I will not."

" Yes, you shall!" And the husband dragged her after him.

When he got her well into the woods he placed her upon a rough table, he had constructed, and cut off her arms and legs. Then the wife wriggled her body about and sang: " Oh, if I had never married, I could never have come to this."

The husband left her, and returned to his town, telling the people that his wife had gone to visit her relations.

Now a hunter happened to hear the wife's song, and was greatly shocked to find her in such a terrible condition. He returned to town, and told his wife all about it, but cautioned her to tell no one.

But the prince got to hear about it, and knocked his chin-gongo (or bell), and thus summoned all his people together. When they were all assembled, he bade them go and fetch the wife. And they went and brought her, but she died just as she arrived in town.

Then they tied up the husband and accused him of the crime. And while they placed the wife upon a grill, to smoke and dry the body, they placed the husband beneath, in the fire, and so burnt him.

X.

THE WONDERFUL CHILD.

A MAN had two wives named Kengi and Gunga. One day he called them to him, and said that he was going to Loango to buy salt, and so might be away some time. He left them both well. Some time after he had gone, Kengi became heavy with child. And Gunga asked her how it was that she was in that condition.

" It is true," said Kengi, " that I am with child; but never you mind. When the child is born, you will see that it is his."

" How can it be, when he has been gone so long ? " rejoined Gunga.

Now when the child was born, it carried with it a handful of hair. And all the people marvelled. Then the child spoke, and said: " This is the work of God."

And the people ran away, they were so much afraid. And when the child grew up, he went into the woods to hunt elephants. And all this time the father had not returned.

One day the child killed an elephant, and came to tell his mother of his good fortune. They called the princes together; and then they went and cut up the elephant and divided it among the people. Then the people said that he was a good child.

And now the father returned, and Kengi was afraid, and prayed Gunga not to tell him that the child was his.

" No, I will not, Kengi," said Gunga; " but the boy himself will."

And when the father came the boy went up to him, and said: " Father, give me your hand."

" Nay, child, I know thee not.   If I am thy father, tell me, child, when did I give thee birth, and by whom ? "

And the people all said : " He is your son by Kengi."

" Nay, I left Kengi well."

Then the son sings: " Now am I indeed dead, and become a bird."

And hearing this, the father took his son to his heart, and gave him a wife, and made him chief over many towns.

XI.

HOW KENGI LOST HER CHILD.

Nenpetro had two wives, Kengi and Gunga. So he cleared a piece of ground for them, and divided it, giving each her part. And they planted maize, and beans, and cassava; and soon they had plenty to eat.

One day Gunga took some beans from Kengi's plantation, and this made Kengi very cross. Gunga was sorry that she had done wrong, but pointed out that they were both married to one man, and that they ate together. After some time they came to an agreement that all that was born on the farm of the one should belong exclusively to her, and that the other should have no right to take it for her use.

Some time after this Kengi came to Gunga's plantation, and asked her for a little tobacco, as she was in great pain and wished to smoke. Gunga told her to sit down awhile, and gave her tobacco. And while Kengi was on Gunga's plantation, she bore a child. Gunga took possession of the child, and would not give it up to Kengi. Kengi wept bitterly, and sent a special ambassador to Gunga demanding her child. But Gunga refused to give the child up, and said she was ready to hold a palaver over it. Thus the two women resolved to go to the town of Manilombi and state their grievance to him.

They arrived, and Manilombi received their presents, and welcomed them. He then asked them what ailed them.

Kengi said: " I brought forth a child. Gunga has robbed me of it; let her speak."

And Gunga answered: " Nay, the child is mine; for when I took some beans from Kengi's plantation, Kengi got vexed, and made me come to an agreement with her that whatsoever was born on her plantation should belong to her, and all that was born on my plantation should belong to me, and neither of us should take anything from each other's plantation. Now, Kengi came, uncalled by me, to my plantation, and this child was born there; so that, according to our agreement, the child is mine and she cannot take it from me."

And witnesses were called, and they gave their evidence.

Then the prince and his old men went to drink water. And when they returned, Manilombi said that Gunga was acting within her right, and that therefore the child should belong to her.

XII.

THE TWIN BROTHERS.

A certain woman, after prolonged labour, gave birth to twins, both sons. And each one, as he was brought forth, came into this world with a valuable fetish, or charm. One the mother called Luemba, the other Mavungu. And they were almost full-grown at their birth, so that Mavungu, the first-born, wished to start upon his travels.

Now about this time the daughter of Nzambi was ready for marriage. The tiger came and offered himself in marriage; but Nzambi told him that he must speak to her daughter himself, as she should only marry the man of her choice. Then the tiger went to the girl and asked her to marry him, but she refused him. And the gazelle, and the pig, and all created things that had breath, one after the other, asked the daughter in marriage; but she refused them all, saying that she did not love them; and they were all very sad.

Mavungu heard of this girl, and determined to marry her. And so he called upon his charm, and asked him to help him; and then he took some grass in his hands, and changed one blade of grass into a horn, another into a knife, another into a gun, and so on, until he was quite ready for the long journey.

Then he set out, and travelled and travelled, until at last hunger overcame him, when he asked his charm whether it was true that he was going to be allowed to starve. The charm hastened to place a sumptuous feast before him, and Mavungu ate and was satisfied.

" Oh, charm !" Mavungu said, " are you going to leave these beautiful plates which I have used for the use of any commoner that may come along ?" The charm immediately caused all to disappear.

Then Mavungu travelled and travelled, until at length he became very tired, and had to ask his charm to arrange a place for him where he might sleep. And the charm saw to his comfort, so that he passed a peaceful night.

And after many days' weary travelling he at length arrived at Nzambi's town. And Nzambi's daughter saw Mavungu and straightway fell in love with him, and ran to her mother and father and cried : " I have seen the man I love, and I shall die if I do not marry him."

Then Mavungu sought out Nzambi, and told her that he had come to marry her daughter.

" Go and see her first," said Nzambi, " and if she will have you, you may marry her."

And when Mavungu and the daughter of Nzambi saw each other, they ran towards each other and loved one another.

And they were led to a fine shimbec ; and whilst all the people in the town danced and sang for gladness, Mavungu and the daughter of Nzambi slept there. And in the morning Mavungu noticed that the whole shimbec was crowded with mirrors, but that each mirror was covered so that the glass could not be seen. And he asked the daughter of Nzambi to uncover them, so that he might see himself in them. And she took him to one and opened it, and Mavungu immediately saw the perfect likeness of his native town. And she took him to another, and he there saw another town he knew; and thus she took him to all the mirrors save one, and this one she refused to let him see.

"Why will you not let me look into that mirror?" asked Mavungu.

"Because that is the picture of the town whence no man that wanders there returns."

"Do let me see it!" urged Mavungu.

At last the daughter of Nzambi yielded, and Mavungu looked hard at the reflected image of that terrible place.

"I must go there," he said.

"Nay, you will never return. Please don't go!" pleaded the daughter of Nzambi.

"Have no fear!" answered Mavungu. "My charm will protect me."

The daughter of Nzambi cried very much, but could not move Mavungu from his purpose. Mavungu then left his newly-married wife, and mounted his horse, and set off for the town from whence no man returns.

He travelled and travelled, until at last he came near to the town, when, meeting an old woman, he asked her for fire to light his pipe.

"Tie up your horse first, and come and fetch it."

Mavungu descended, and having tied his horse up very securely, he went to the woman for the fire; and when he had come near to her she killed him, so that he disappeared entirely.

Now Luemba wondered at the long absence of his brother Mavungu, and determined to follow him. So he took some grass, and by the aid of his fetish changed one blade into a horse, another into a knife, another into a gun, and so on, until he was fully prepared for his journey. Then he set out, and after some days' journeying arrived at Nzambi's town.

Nzambi rushed out to meet him, and, calling him Mavungu, embraced him.

"Nay," said Luemba, "my name is not Mavungu; I am his brother, Luemba."

"Nonsense!" answered Nzambi. "You are my son-in-law, Mavungu." And straightway a great feast was prepared. Nzambi's daughter danced for joy, and would not hear of his not being Mavungu. And Luemba was sorely troubled, and did not know what to do, as he was now sure that Nzambi's daughter was Mavungu's wife. And when night came, Nzambi's daughter would sleep in Luemba's shimbec; but he appealed to his charm, and it enclosed Nzambi's daughter in a room, and lifted her out of Luemba's room for the night, bringing her back in the early morning.

And Luemba's curiosity was aroused by the many closed mirrors that hung about the walls; so he asked Nzambi's daughter to let him look into them. And she showed him all excepting one; and this she told him was the one that reflected the town whence no man returns. Luemba insisted upon looking into this one; and when he had seen the terrible picture he knew that his brother was there.

Luemba determined to leave Nzambi's town for the town whence no man returns; and so after thanking them all for his kind reception, he set out. They all wept loudly, but were consoled by the fact that he had been there once already, and returned safely, so that he could of course return a second time. And Luemba travelled and travelled, until he also came to where the old woman was standing, and asked her for fire.

She told him to tie up his horse and come to her to fetch it, but he tied his horse up only very lightly, and then fell upon the old woman and killed her.

Then he sought out his brother's bones and the bones of his horse, and put them together, and then touched them with his charm. And Mavungu and his horse came to life again. Then together they joined the bones of hundreds of people together and touched them with their charms, so that they all lived again. And then they set off with all their followers to Nzambi's town. And Luemba told Mavungu how he had been mistaken for him by his father-in-law and wife, and how by the help of his charm he had saved his wife from dishonour; and Mavungu thanked him, and said it was well.

Then a quarrel broke out between the two brothers about the followers. Mavungu said they were his, because he was the elder; but Luemba said that they belonged to him, because he had given Mavungu and them all life. Mavungu then fell upon Luemba and killed him; but his horse remained by his body. Mavungu then went on his way to Nzambi's town, and was magnificently welcomed.

Now Luemba's horse took his charm and touched Luemba's body, so that he lived again. Then Luemba mounted his horse, and sought out his brother Mavungu and killed him.

And when the town had heard the palaver, they all said that Luemba had done quite rightly.

XIII.

THE YOUNGER BROTHER WHO KNEW MORE THAN THE ELDER.

In a certain town there lived two brothers who could not agree with one another, the younger continually asserting that he knew more than his brother, thus enraging his elder.

At last the younger brother said he could stand it no longer, and threatened to leave his town. So he and his wife left the the town and wandered far away, until at last they entered a wood and came to a little river of very clear water.

"Let us drink," he said, "and sit down here, as there does not seem to be a path leading from the river on the other side."

So they drank and rested. Then he got up and waded down the stream some way, and found a pathway on the other side of the river. He called his wife, and they proceeded on their way. Soon they heard voices, and wondered what kind of people could have built in such a place.

"Let us go back," said the wife; "how do you know that these people will not harm us?"

"Nay, I will not go back; so let us enter the town at once." They saw only two or three huts.

Now these huts, or shimbees, were inhabited by a man and his

F

wife, who had left his town on account of certain "palavers" that had been constantly pushed against him.

"And where do you come from?" said he, as the stranger and his wife entered his clearing.

The younger brother told him how it was that he had left his town and wandered there, and added that he would like to live there with him.

"Very well, you can do so.   But first tell me, are you a bad man?"

"No, certainly not; I am a good man, the others treated me badly."

"Well, there's a shimbec for you; stay there."

They did nothing for four days; but on the fifth day the man proposed that they should take their women with their hoes to a certain place he knew of, and get them to dig a large hole, which they would cover over with dried sticks and leaves, so as to form a trap for the many wild animals that passed that way. This they did.

"Now, that we may not quarrel over the game we catch, tell me: which will you have, the males or the females?"

The younger brother said he would take the males.

"Agreed!   Then I will take the females."

"Agreed!"

They went back to their towns, and slept soundly that night. The next morning very early they went to see their trap.   They had caught an ox.

"'Tis yours," said the owner of the town, "take it."

The next day an antelope, the next day a chimbimbi,* and

* A kind of antelope-mouse coloured with a fawn-coloured patch on its shoulders and back, small straight horns like a goat.

the next a hog, each day a male of some kind, until the younger brother had so much meat that he did not know what to do with it. But he gave the owner of the town none of it. He sent his wife out into the woods to gather sticks to smoke the meat, and so preserve it. Towards night he became anxious about her, as she had not returned. He went to the owner of the town and told him about it. But he could not account for her absence.

" Let us go and look for her."

" Nay," said the man, " it is night. To-morrow we will go."

The younger brother roamed about the whole night, crying and moaning at the loss of his wife. Early he awoke the owner of the town and asked him to go with him to look for her.

" Yes. But first let us go and see the trap, for I have dreamt that luck has changed, and that to-day we shall catch a female."

They went, and soon discovered the female in the trap. It was the young man's wife. Overjoyed at finding her the young man wanted to jump into the hole to help her out. But the man reminded him of his agreement, and how he had given him nothing of all the meat he had entrapped.

" Nay, take all the meat you like, but my wife is a human being, surely you will not kill and eat her ? "

" She is mine by agreement, I can do as I like with her." And thus they went on wrangling the day through.

Now the elder brother had gone out hunting and had chanced to come into the wood not far from where the trap was. He heard voices, and so crept cautiously up in that direction. He recognised his brother's voice and ran to him. The younger brother was overjoyed to see him and welcomed him boisterously. The elder brother met him coldly. When the owner of the town knew who the stranger was, he laid the whole matter before him, and asked him to say whether the female in the trap was his or not. The elder heard all, and answered that the female in the trap was certainly his, and that he had better go in and kill her. The younger brother tried to restrain him ; but the man flung him aside and jumped into the trap.

"Fool," said the elder to the younger, when he saw him trying to stop the man from entering the pit; "can you not yet trust your brother's superior wisdom? See, now, that male in your trap; he is yours by agreement, even as your wife is his. Spare his life, and perhaps he will give you back your wife." The man saw how he had been fooled, and gave the woman up. The two brothers and the wife then returned to their town.

XIV.

THE CHIMPANZEE AND GORILLA.

A NATIVE friend of mine, who considers himself a great hunter and naturalist, told me that, his plantations having suffered severely from the depredations of the gorilla, he had determined to follow up his tracks, and kill him, if possible. After having journeyed a long distance, he at last came up to the gorilla's camp. The gorilla was up a tree, at the foot of which was a large heap of fruits of different kinds. He resolved upon the bold course of getting as near this fruit as he could, waiting until the gorilla should come down. Hardly had he got himself safely in his chosen position, when a chimpanzee, club in hand, came leisurely along, evidently looking about for food.

"Oh la! What fool has left his food in such a place, I wonder, right in the public footpath? I need go no further."

Thereupon the chimpanzee sat himself down, and began to enjoy a really good feed. He had not been there very long, however, before the gorilla came quietly down the tree. He quietly seated himself opposite to the chimpanzee, and commenced to eat also.

"Here, you!" said the chimpanzee, "what do you mean by eating my fruit? Can't you go and find some for yourself?"

The gorilla made no reply, but went on eating. The chimpanzee got excited, and began to abuse the gorilla. The gorilla looked at him. Then the chimpanzee struck the gorilla. The gorilla smiled, and pushed him aside. The chimpanzee took his club, and hit the gorilla with all his might. The gorilla then raised his long arm, and gave the chimpanzee one fearful blow, which stretched him dead at his feet.

"I did not wait to see any more," said my friend, "but ran away as hard as I could."

XV.

THE ANTELOPE AND THE LEOPARD.

THE leopard one day bet his life to the antelope, that if he hid himself the antelope would never find him.

" Well," said the antelope, " I accept your bet. Go and hide yourself."

And the leopard went into the woods and hid himself. Then the antelope looked for him, and after a little while found him. And the leopard was very angry with the antelope, and told him to go and hide himself, and see how easily he would find him. The antelope agreed to this, but told the leopard that he would have his life.

After some time the leopard set out to seek the antelope. He searched the woods through and through, but could not find him. At last, thoroughly worn out, he sat down, saying : " I am too fat to walk any more ; and I am also very hungry. I will pick some of these nonje nuts, and carry them to my town and eat them."

So he filled the bag he carried under his arm (called *nkutu*), and returned to his town. Once there, he determined to call his people together, and continue his search for the antelope after breakfast.

So he knocked his ngongo, and ordered all his people to assemble, from the babe that was born yesterday, to the sick men who could not walk and must be carried in a hammock. When they were all there, he ordered his slaves to crack the nonje nuts. But out of the first nut that they cracked jumped a beautiful dog.

Now, the leopard was married to four princesses. To one by common consent, to another by the rites of Boomba, to the third by the rites of Funzi, and to the fourth by those of Lembe. Each of his wives had her own cooking-shed.

Now, when the little dog jumped out of the nut, it ran into the first wife's shed. She beat it, so that it ran away and entered the shed of the wife after the rites of Boomba. This wife also beat the dog, so that it took refuge with the wife after the rites of Funzi. She also beat the little dog; and thus it fled to the wife after the rites of Lembe. She killed it.

But as the dog was dying, it changed into a beautiful damsel. And when the leopard saw this beautiful maiden, he longed to marry her, and straightway asked her to be his wife.

The beautiful girl answered him and said: " First, kill those four women who killed the little dog."

The leopard immediately killed them. Then the maid said: " How can I marry a man with such dreadful-looking nails. Please have them taken out."

The leopard was so much in love with the maiden, that he had his claws drawn.

" What fearful eyes you have got, my dear leopard ! I can never live with you with those eyes always looking at me. Please take them out."

The leopard sighed, but obeyed.

"I never saw such ugly ears; why don't you have them cut?"
The leopard had them cut.

"You have certainly the clumsiest feet that have been seen in this world! Can you not have them chopped off?"

The leopard in despair had his feet taken off.

"And now my dear, dear leopard, there is but one more favour that I have to ask you. Have you not noticed how ugly your teeth are? how they disfigure you? Please have them drawn."

The leopard was now very weak, but he was so fascinated by the girl, and so hopeful now that he would obtain her by this last sacrifice, that he sent to the cooking-shed for a stone and had his teeth knocked out.

The maiden then saw that the leopard was fast dying. So she turned herself into the antelope, and thus addressed him:

"My dear leopard, you thought to kill me to avoid giving your life to me, as promised, when I found you. See now how I have outdone you. I have destroyed you and your whole family." And this is why the leopard now always kills the antelope when he meets one.

XVI.

HOW THE SPIDER WON AND LOST NZAMBI'S DAUGHTER.

Nzambi on earth had a beautiful daughter ; but she swore that no earthly being should marry her, who could not bring her the heavenly fire from Nzambi Mpungu, who dwelt in the heavens above the blue roof. And as the daughter was very fair to look upon, the people marvelled, saying : " How shall we secure this treasure ? and who on such a condition will ever marry her ? ".

Then the spider said: " I will, if you will help me."

And they all answered : " We will gladly help you, if you will reward us."

Then the spider reached the blue roof of heaven, and dropped down again to the earth, leaving a strong silken thread firmly hanging from the roof to the earth below. Now, he called the tortoise, the woodpecker, the rat, and the sandfly, and bade them climb up the thread to the roof. And they did so. Then the woodpecker pecked a hole through the roof, and they all entered the realm of the badly dressed Nzambi Mpungu.*

Nzambi Mpungu received them courteously, and asked them what they wanted up there.

* *See* Appendix, p. 133.

And they answered him, saying : " O Nzambi Mpungu of the heavens above, great father of all the world, we have come to fetch some of your terrible fire, for Nzambi who rules upon earth."

" Wait here then," said Nzambi Mpungu, " while I go to my people and tell them of the message that you bring."

But the sandfly unseen accompanied Nzambi Mpungu and heard all that was said. And while he was gone, the others wondered if it were possible for one who went about so poorly clad to be so powerful.

Then Nzambi Mpungu returned to them, and said : " My friend, how can I know that you have really come from the ruler of the earth, and that you are not impostors ? "

" Nay," they said; "put us to some test that we may prove our sincerity to you."

" I will," said Nzambi Mpungu. " Go down to this earth of yours, and bring me a bundle of bamboos, that I may make myself a shed."

And the tortoise went down, leaving the others where they were, and soon returned with the bamboos.

Then Nzambi Mpungu said to the rat : "Get thee beneath this bundle of bamboos, and I will set fire to it. Then if thou escape I shall surely know that Nzambi sent you."

And the rat did as he was bidden. And Nzambi Mpungu set fire to the bamboos, and lo ! when they were entirely consumed, the rat came from amidst the ashes unharmed.

Then he said: " You are indeed what you represent your-selves to be. I will go and consult my people again."

Then they sent the sandfly after him, bidding him to keep well out of sight, to hear all that was said, and if possible to find out where the lightning was kept. The midge returned and related all that he had heard and seen.

Then Nzambi Mpungu returned to them, and said: "Yes, I will give you the fire you ask for, if you can tell me where it is kept."

And the spider said : " Give me then, O Nzambi Mpungu, one of the five cases that you keep in the fowl-house."

" Truly you have answered me correctly, O spider! Take therefore this case, and give it to your Nzambi."

And the tortoise carried it down to the earth; and the spider presented the fire from heaven to Nzambi; and Nzambi gave the spider her beautiful daughter in marriage.

But the woodpecker grumbled, and said : "Surely the woman is mine; for it was I who pecked the hole through the roof, without which the others never could have entered the kingdom of the Nzambi Mpungu above."

" Yes," said the rat, " but see how I risked my life among the burning bamboos; the girl, I think, should be mine."

" Nay, O Nzambi ; the girl should certainly be mine; for without my help the others would never have found out where the fire was kept," said the sandfly.

Then Nzambi said : " Nay, the spider undertook to bring me the fire; and he has brought it. The girl by rights is his; but as you others will make her life miserable if I allow her to live with the spider, and I cannot give her to you all, I will give her to none, but will give you each her market value."

Nzambi then paid each of them fifty longs of cloth and one case of gin ; and her daughter remained a maiden and waited upon her mother for the rest of her days.

XVII.

THE TURTLE AND THE MAN.

A TURTLE and a man built themselves a small town, but because they had as yet planted nothing they suffered from hunger.

"Let us build a large trap," said the turtle, "that we may catch an antelope." The man agreed, and they set to work and made a very large one.

"This is too large," said the turtle, "let us divide it, and each have a trap of his own."

The man divided it and the turtle chose the best one. That night the man caught nothing, but a splendid antelope was found in the turtle's trap. As the turtle could not lift it, he called all the people from round about to a dance.

While they were dancing, the chimpacasi, or wild ox, came out of the wood and wanted to know what all this singing was about. And the turtle told him that he had caught an antelope, and as he could not carry it to his house, he had called in his friends. "Perhaps, good ox, you will take the antelope out of the trap for me and lift it as far as my house."

"Oh, certainly," said the ox.

"And now, please go and fetch some water."

The ox went and drew some water. They then cut up the antelope.

" Clean the plates, please," said the turtle.

And the delighted ox washed them.

" This is your share, dear ox ; but you must go and get some leaves to wrap it in."

And while the ox was away in the woods, collecting leaves, the turtle lifted all the meat up and carried it into his house, which was a very strong one, and shut himself inside.

The ox returned and asked for his share, but the turtle refused to let him have it, and insulted him grossly.   The ox became very angry, and told the turtle that he would destroy the trap.   But the turtle had reset the trap, so that when the ox put his head in he was caught, and died after a short struggle.

" Oh, oh, Mr. Ox, I told you so.   You should be more careful when you are entering the turtle's trap."

He called the people again to dance and sing.

This time the leopard was attracted by the noise, and came to the turtle to find out what it was all about.   And the turtle told him, and said that his hands were very sore, and that he could not carry the ox to his house : would the leopard drag him there ?

Glad to oblige the turtle, the leopard at once offered his services, and in a very short time had brought the ox to the turtle's house.

" Thank you, dear leopard, will you now go to the river and fetch some water, and clean the pots ? "

" Certainly," said the leopard.

And when they had cooked the whole of the ox, the turtle put aside part of the meat for the leopard, and carried the rest into his shimbec.

" You would better go and fetch some leaves to wrap the meat in," said the turtle.

The leopard went. While he was away, the turtle took the meat, and shut himself within his strong house.

The leopard returned and said : " Turtle, turtle, where is my meat ? "

" It is here, my dear leopard."

" Then give it me."

" Nay, the ox was mine."

" Yes, but I helped you to cook it."

" Well, I shall not give you any."

" Then I will destroy your trap."

" Take care you do not meet with the fate of the ox."

" Yes, I will take care."

And the leopard went and destroyed the trap entirely, and then, placing the rope round his neck lay down in the middle of the ruins, as if he had been entrapped.

Then the turtle went again to look at his trap and was delighted to find the leopard there.

" Ah, ah, I told you so ! Why did you not take more care, my dear leopard ? "

And the turtle stretched out his long neck as if to kiss the leopard. The leopard sprang upon him, and bit the turtle's head off before he had time to pull it in. He then entered his shimbec and ate up all the meat that the turtle had stored there.

Now the man wondered what the leopard was doing in the turtle's shimbec. So he went there and asked the leopard And the leopard told him how the turtle had tried to trick him, and how he had killed the turtle. And the man said he was quite right and might go on eating the food of the turtle.

XVIII.

KILLING A LEOPARD.

I CLOSED the autobiography of a Fjort in " Seven Years among the Fjort" thus: " We were obliged to hurry back to town, however, as notice was brought to us that some one had killed a leopard. The custom is that when a leopard is killed, the people of the different towns in that district can loot each other's towns to their hearts' content, and on the day fixed for the delivery of the leopard to the king, the destroyer of the leopard can take it through any of the towns he chooses, having the right to appropriate any article he may meet in his road that is not inside a shimbec or other dwelling."

I can now tell you more of this custom. The slayer, it seems, is himself tied up, and the head of the leopard is carefully wrapped up in cloth. Both are then taken to the king, who addresses the slayer thus :

" My son, why have you slain this man ? "

" Father," answers the slayer, " he is a very dangerous man and has taken the life of many of your people's sheep and fowls."

" Thou hast done well, my son. Count now the hairs of his whiskers. As thou knowest, there should be three times nine hairs, and for every one that is missing must thou pay me two pieces of cloth."

" Father, they are all there."

" Then pull them out carefully; take also his teeth, his claws, and his skin, and prepare them for my use."

This the hunter does and presents them to the king.

Then the king again addresses him :

" My son, thou art a great hunter and must need someone to cook thy food for thee when thou goest out hunting. Take therefore this young girl as thy slave, or concubine."

" But father, look ! I am not in a fit state to receive such a gift; my clothes are worn and tattered."

" Thou sayest but what is the truth, my son. Take therefore these clothes and dress thyself."

" Yea, father, thou art too good to me; but I have no one to cut wood for such a beautiful creature."

" There, there, take this small boy to cut wood for her, and this man to carry thy gun."

" I clap my hands to thee, father, and thank thee."

Then the king has to give a grand feast in honour of the event.

XIX.

THE GAZELLE AND THE LEOPARD.

THE gazelle said to the leopard : " It is now the dry season, and we should be cutting down the bush, that our women may plant as soon as the first rains come."

" Well," said the leopard, " I cannot go to-day, but you may as well go."

And the gazelle went ; and all that day he cut the bush, and cleared the ground for planting. And the next day he went also alone.

On the third day the leopard called on the gazelle and asked him to go to the plantation with him. But the gazelle said he was sick, and could not go, so the leopard went by himself.

The next day the leopard again called for the gazelle, but he was not in.

" Where has he gone ?" enquired the leopard.

" Oh, he has gone to another part."

And each day the leopard called upon the gazelle he was either sick or out of town ; so that the leopard had nearly all the hard work to himself. When the women had planted, and the harvest was ripe, however, the gazelle went to look at the plantation. He was greatly pleased to find so much planted, and thought how pleased his friends would be if he invited them to a feast; so he called in all the antelopes and other beasts of the field, and they had a splendid feast.

By and by the leopard thought he would go and see how his plantation was getting on, and no sooner had he arrived there than he exclaimed: "Hullo, who has been feeding on my plantation and eaten up my corn? Surely I will set a trap for them and catch the thieves."

The next day the animals, led by the little gazelle, came again; and he warned them, saying: "Be careful, for the leopard will surely set a trap for us." But the antelope became careless, and finally fell into the leopard's trap. "There," says the gazelle, "I told you to be careful. What shall we do? They have all run away and left us, and I am not strong enough to release you."

Then the leopard came, and rejoiced greatly at having caught a thief. He took the antelope to his town. "Please, Sir, the gazelle told me to go," cried the antelope, "don't kill me, don't kill me."

"How am I to catch the gazelle?" the leopard replied. "No, I must kill you." And so he killed the antelope and ate him.

When the gazelle heard what the leopard had done, he was greatly annoyed, and declared that as the leopard was their chief, they were quite right in eating the food he had provided for them. Was it not the duty of the father to provide for his children? "Well, well, never mind, he will pay us for this."

Then the gazelle made a drum, and beat it until all the animals came as if to a dance. When they were assembled, he told them that they must be revenged upon the leopard.

The leopard heard the drum, and said to his wife: "Let us

go to the dance." But his wife said she would rather stay at home, and did not go. The leopard went; but no sooner had he arrived than they all set upon him and killed him. And when the dance was over, the leopard's wife wondered why he did not return. The gazelle sent her the head of her husband skinned as her part of the feast; and not knowing that it was her husband's head, she ate it.

"Oh, for shame," said the gazelle, "You have eaten your husband's head."

"Nay, Sir, the shame rests with you; for you gave it to me to eat, after having murdered him." And she wept and cursed the gazelle.

XX.

THE WILD CAT AND THE GAZELLE.

NENPETRO (kind of wild cat) and Nsessi (the gazelle), agreed that in case of famine the one might eat the other's mother. The famine came. Nsessi killed Nenpetro's mother and ate her; but, loving his own mother very much, he took her into the bush, and hid her there in a cave, telling her never to come out unless she should hear him call her. Each day he took her food, but not caring to carry it himself, he got Nenpetro's little son to carry it for him.

Now this little boy felt with his father in his loss of his mother, and so resolved to tell him where Nsessi kept his mother. Thus he told Nenpetro, and showed him the way to the cave where Nsessi had hidden his mother. Nenpetro then simulated the voice of Nsessi, and called to her to come out. When she came, Nenpetro killed her and took her to town. Then he had her cooked, and gave a feast, and invited Nsessi. But Nsessi wondered where he could have got his meat, and went to look for his mother. Could he have killed her? She was not there. Yes, he had killed her. He refused Nenpetro's invitation, and said he would no longer live in that town. So he called his people together, and they burned their houses and went to live elsewhere.

XXI

THE CRAFTY WOMAN OVERREACHES HERSELF.

It was market day, and all were intent upon going to Kitanda (the market). The first lady to arrive brought a large basket of chicoanga (native bread), placed it under the shade of the market-tree, and then hid herself in the bush near at hand.

A second lady came along with a basket (or matet) of pig, and sat herself down beneath the tree.

" I wonder," said she, as she caught sight of the chicoanga, " to whom that belongs ? I should very much like one piece to eat with a little of my pig. I was so busy preparing the pig for market, that I really had no time to get any chicoanga ready." She raised her voice and cried out :

" To whom does this chicoanga belong ? Where is its owner ? "

This she repeated many times, and then came to the conclusion that it had no owner. So she took one piece and ate it with her pig.

By-and-bye the owner of the chicoanga came forth, and told the owner of the pig that she must pay her in pig for the chicoanga she had taken.

" No," said the owner of the pig.

And the people round about were called in ; and after hearing what both had to say, they declared that the woman who owned the chicoanga was in the wrong; because she had hidden herself in the bush on purpose that her chicoanga should be taken by the owner of the pig, whom she had evidently seen coming. She had laid this trap to get some of the pig, and she deserved to lose her chicoanga.

XXII

HOW THE FETISH SUNGA PUNISHED MY GREAT-UNCLE'S TWIN BROTHER, BASA.

BASA was my great uncle's twin brother, and a very clever fisherman. Every day he used to go out fishing in the river; and every day he caught great quantities of fish, which he used to smuggle into his house, so that none should know that he had caught any. His brother and relations used each day to ask him: " Basa, have you caught any fish ? " And he would answer " No," although his house was full of fish going rotten. All this time the fetish Sunga was watching, and was grieved to hear him lie thus. So one day she sent one of her moleques, or little servants, to the place where Basa was fishing, to call him to her. It happened that upon that day Basa caught so much fish that he had to make some new matets, or baskets, to hold it all. He had already filled two, and placed them in the fork of a large tree, when he heard three distinct clappings of the hands, as if some child were saluting him, and then he heard a voice saying: " Come to my mother."

Then Basa was greatly afraid, and answered: " Which way ? please show me the way."

" Follow me," said the voice of the child, as she led him to the river.

When they stepped into the river, the waters dried up, and all the fish disappeared, so that the bed of the river formed a perfect road for them. Even the fallen trees had been removed, that Basa might not meet the slightest difficulty in the way. When they had reached the watershed of the river, there in the great lake he saw a large and beautiful town. Here he was met by many people, and warmly welcomed. They led him to a chair, and asked him to be seated. But he was alarmed at all this ceremony, and wondered what it all meant.

Then Sunga laid a table before him, and loaded it with food and wine, and asked him to eat and drink. But he was still afraid, and told Sunga that so grand was the feast she had placed before him that the smell alone of it had satisfied him. Then she pressed him to eat and drink, and finally he did so, drinking all the wine that there was.

Then Sunga deprived him of the power of speech, that he might lie no more, and bade him depart to his town. And so for the future he could only make his wants known by signs.

XXIII.

THE RABBIT AND THE ANTELOPE.

It was during an almost rainless "hot season," when all who had no wells were beginning to feel the pangs of thirst, that the rabbit and the antelope formed a partnership to dig a deep well so that they could never be in want of water.

"Let us finish our food," said the antelope, "and be off to our work."

"Nay," said the rabbit; "had we not better keep the food for later on, when we are tired and hungry after our work?"

"Very well, hide the food, rabbit; and let us get to work, I am very thirsty."

They arrived at the place where they purposed having the well, and worked hard for a short time.

"Listen!" said the rabbit; "they are calling me to go back to town."

"Nay, I do not hear them."

"Yes, they are certainly calling me, and I must be off. My wife is about to present me with some children, and I must name them."

"Go then, dear rabbit, but come back as soon as you can."

The rabbit ran off to where he had hidden the food, and ate some of it, and then went back to his work.

" Well!" said the antelope, "what have you called your little one ?"

" Uncompleted one," said the rabbit.

" A strange name," said the antelope.

Then they worked for a while.

" Again they are calling me," cried the rabbit. " I must be off, so please excuse me. Cannot you hear them calling me ?"

" No," said the antelope, " I hear nothing."

Away ran the rabbit, leaving the poor antelope to do all the work, while he ate some more of the food that really belonged to them both. When he had had enough, he hid the food again, and ran back to the well.

" And what have you called your last, rabbit ?"

" Half-completed one."

" What a funny little fellow you are! But come, get on with the digging; see how hard I have worked."

Then they worked hard for quite a long time. " Listen, now !" said the rabbit, " surely you heard them calling me this time!"

" Nay, dear rabbit, I can hear nothing; but go, and get back quickly."

Away ran the rabbit, and this time he finished the food before going back to his work.

" Well, little one, what have you called your third child ?"

" Completed," answered the rabbit. Then they worked hard and as night was setting in returned to their village.

" I am terribly tired, rabbit; run and get the food, or I shall faint."

The rabbit went to look for the food, and then calling out to the antelope, told him that some horrid cat must have been there, as the food was all gone, and the pot quite clean. The antelope groaned, and went hungry to bed.

The next day the naughty little rabbit played the antelope the same trick. And the next day he again tricked the antelope. And the next, and the next, until at last the antelope accused the rabbit of stealing the food. Then the rabbit got angry, and dared him to take casca (or the test-bark, a purge or emetic).

"Let us both take it," said the antelope, "and let him whose tail is the first to become wet, be considered the guilty one."

So they took the casca and went to bed. And as the medicine began to take effect upon the rabbit, he cried out to the antelope :

" See, your tail is wet ! "

" Nay, it is not ! "

" Yes, it is ! "

" No, but yours is, dear rabbit ; see there ! "

Then the rabbit feared greatly, and tried to run away. But the antelope said : " Fear not, rabbit ; I will do you no harm. Only you must promise not to drink of the water of my well, and to leave my company for ever."

Accordingly the rabbit left him and went his way.

Some time after this, a bird told the antelope that the rabbit used to drink the water of the well every day. Then the antelope was greatly enraged, and determined to kill the rabbit. So the antelope laid a trap for the silly little rabbit. He cut a piece of wood, and shaped it into the figure of an animal about the size of the rabbit ; and then he placed this figure firmly in the ground near to the well, and smeared it all over with bird-lime.

The rabbit went as usual to drink the waters of the well, and was much annoyed to find an animal there, as he thought, drinking the water also.

"And what may you be doing here, Sir?" said the rabbit to the figure.

The figure answered not.

Then the rabbit, thinking that it was afraid of him, went close up to it, and again asked what he was doing there.

But the figure made no answer.

"What!" said the rabbit, "do you mean to insult me? Answer me at once, or I will strike you."

The figure answered not.

Then the little rabbit lifted up his right hand, and smacked the figure in the face. His hand stuck to the figure.

"What's the matter?" said the rabbit. "Let my hand go, sir, at once, or I will hit you again."

The figure held fast to the rabbit's right hand. Then the rabbit hit the figure a swinging blow with his left. The left hand stuck to the figure also.

"What can be the matter with you, Sir? You are excessively silly. Let my hands go at once, or I will kick you."

And the rabbit kicked the figure with his right foot; but his right foot stuck there. Then he got into a great rage, and kicked the figure with his left. And his left leg stuck to the figure also. Then, overcome with rage, he bumped the figure with his head and stomach, but these parts also stuck to the figure. Then the rabbit cried with impotent rage. The antelope, just about this time, came along to drink water; and when he saw the rabbit helplessly fastened to the figure, he laughed at him, and then killed him.

XXIV

THE FIGHT BETWEEN THE TWO FETISHES, LIFUMA AND CHIMPUKELA.

Now this is a sad but true story, for it is of recent occurrence, and many living witnesses can vouch for its truth.

Poor King Jack, late of Cabinda, now retired a little into the interior of KaCongo, known to all who visit this part of Africa, either in whaler, steamer, or man of war, owns the fetish called Lifuma. Lifuma had all his life sniffed the fresh sea-breezes, and rejoiced with his people when they returned from the deep sea in their canoes laden with fish. But now circumstances (namely, the occupation of Cabinda by the Portuguese) forced him to retire to the interior, behind the coast-line between Futilla and Cabinda. How he longed to see his people happy yet again is proved by the trouble he put himself to in trying to gain possession of a part of the sea-beach that he thought should belong to his " hinterland." He left the sweet waters of Lake Chinganga Miyengela (waters that have travelled even to the white man's country, and returned without being corrupted) and quietly travelled down to the sea-beach, near to a place called Kaia. Once there, he picked up a few shells and pebbles, and filled a pint mug with salt water, meaning to carry them back to his sweet-water home, and to place them on the holy ground beside him as a sign of his ownership of the sea-beach, and as a means whereby his people might once more play on the sea-beach by the salt water, and once again occupy themselves in fishing in the deep blue sea. Peaceful and benevolent was indeed his mission, and perhaps, as he passed the town of Kaia and Subantanu unmolested, he at last thought that his object was secured. Alas! the bird Ngundu espied him, and rushed to town to acquaint the Kaia people's fetish, called Chimpukela. Then Chimpukela ran after Lifuma, and caught him up, and roughly asked him what he had there, hidden under his cloth.

" Go away," cried the anxious Lifuma, as he pushed Chim-pukela aside.

Chimpukela stumbled over an ant-hill and fell, so that when he got up again he was very angry with Lifuma, and knocked him down. Poor Lifuma fell upon a thorn of the Minyundu tree and broke his leg. The mug of salt water was also spilt, and Chimpukela took from him all the relics he had gathered upon his sea-beach.

Then Chimpukela swore that ant-hills should no longer exist in his country, and that is why you never see one there now as you travel through his country.

And Lifuma cursed the bird Ngundu, and the tree Min-yundu, and canoes, and salt water, and everything pertaining to the beach. And that is why all these things do not now exist in his country, or on his sweet-water lake.

XXV.

THE FETISH OF CHILUNGA.

At a place called Chilunga, north of Loango, there is a fetish called Boio, who by his representative in the flesh, a princess, rules the country with a rod of iron. His dwelling-place is the earth; and as people pass that part which is dedicated to him, they hear his voice. People place their offerings here, and while yet they are looking at them they disappear. The spirit, or fetish, has, besides this human voice, the voice of a certain bird.

The sister of my cook, married to a man in Chilunga, was one day gathering sticks in a wood, when she heard a bird singing very loudly. Half in fun, half seriously, she spoke roughly to it, telling it to keep quiet; when to her astonishment her hands were roughly tied behind her back by some invisible force. She stood rooted to the place, as it were, by fear, and was found there by her husband who, wondering at her delay, had come to look for her.

"How have you angered Boio?" he asked.

She told him what had happened, and said that she did not know that the voice of the bird was that of Boio. The husband ran to the princess, and, having explained the matter, made her a peace-offering. The princess then gave the woman her liberty.

On another occasion some natives laughed at two men who were carrying a hammock-pole as if a hammock was hanging from it. Immediately they were made prisoners by invisible hands, and only released upon a heavy payment being made to the princess by their relations. The men, you see, were carrying the fetish in his hammock, although both it and the hammock were invisible to the passers-by.

Girls who are given in marriage by their parents to ugly men, and who object to them on that account, are taken to the holy ground. Then they hear a voice speaking to them, saying: "Are you then so beautiful that you can afford to despise these good men on account of their ugliness?" Then their hands are tied behind them; and there they remain prisoners until such time as they are willing to marry the men. When the whole town, men, women, and children, go to the holy ground to praise this fetish, it takes a great delight in those who dance well, and punishes those who dance badly.

A certain white man would not believe in the sudden disappearance of the offerings made to this spirit. So he was asked by the princess to come to the holy ground and bring some presents for the spirit. The white man immediately set out with many presents, laughing at the whole matter as if it were a huge joke. His servants placed the gifts upon the ground, while he looked sharply after them. Then they cleared the ground and left him there. And lo! while he was yet looking, the presents disappeared. Then he said he believed in *that* spirit.

Only two men have the power of seeing this fetish in his earthly home; and they are the men appointed to carry food to him.

XXVI

THE LEOPARD AND THE CROCODILE.

ONCE a man and his many wives lived in a certain town far away in the bush. His wives refused to work, and he was at his wit's ends to know what to do to feed them and himself.

One day a happy thought struck him, and away he went into the bush to cut palm-kernels. He cut twenty bunches in all. Then he sought out the leopard, and made him his friend by presenting him with ten bunches of palm-nuts. The leopard thanked him very much, and told him that if he would cut palm-nuts for him, and him only, he would never more be without fresh meat to feed his wives. The man thanked the leopard, and promised to supply his wants.

Then the man went to the crocodile and presented him with ten bunches of palm-nuts. The crocodile was indeed thankful, and promised to supply the man daily with a quantity of fish, if he would only promise in his turn to cut palm-nuts for him and no other.

The next day, the leopard came to the man's town and presented him with a wild pig. The crocodile came soon afterwards and brought him plenty of fish. Thus the town was full of food, and the man and his wives were never hungry.

This continued for a long time, until, in fact, the crocodile and leopard were getting tired of palm-nuts, and asked the man to present them with a dog, as they had heard that dog's flesh was excellent. Hitherto neither the crocodile nor the leopard had met each other, nor had they ever seen a dog. The man did not wish to lose his dogs, so he told them that he had none. But they each day became more anxious to eat dog's flesh, and so they worried the man, until at last he promised them a dog each. But he did not mean to give them the dogs. However, they bothered and vexed him so much that they became a nuisance to him, and he determined to rid himself of them.

The next day, the leopard came and asked for a dog, which as yet he had neither seen nor tasted. The man told him that if he went to such and such a place he would there find a dog just to his taste. The leopard left him to find the dog.

The crocodile also came, bringing plenty of fish, and again asked for a dog. The man told him to go to the same place he had indicated to the leopard, and told him that he would there meet a dog that he would enjoy immensely.

The crocodile arrived at the spot first, but saw nothing that he could imagine a dog. So relying upon the word of the man he closed his eyes and basked in the hot sun. After a time the leopard came along and found the crocodile, as he thought, asleep.

" This is indeed a much larger animal than I had imagined the dog to be," he murmured.

The crocodile, aroused by the rustling noise made by the leopard as he approached, slowly opened his eyes, and thought the leopard was a very large kind of dog, if all he had heard about dogs was true. Hardly had he moved, when the leopard

H 2

sprang upon him.   Then there was a terrible fight, and the
man called all the town to witness it.   After a prolonged
struggle the beasts killed each other, and the man and his
people returned to town and feasted upon the food the crocodile
and leopard had given him, and sang and danced until the
next day.

XXVII.

WHY SOME MEN ARE WHITE AND OTHERS
BLACK.

IT was in the beginning, and four men were walking through
a wood. They came to a place where there were two rivers.
One river was of water, clear as crystal and of great purity;
the other was black and foul and horrible to the taste. And
the four men were puzzled as to which river they should cross;
for, whereas the dirty river seemed more directly in their way,
the clear river was the most pleasant to cross, and perhaps after
they had crossed it they might regain the proper path. The
men, after some consultation, thought that they ought to cross
the black river, and two of them straightway crossed it. The
other two, however, scarce touched and tasted the water than
they hesitated and returned. The two that had now nearly
crossed the river called to them and urged them to come, but in
vain. The other two had determined to leave their companions,
and to cross the beautiful and clear river. They crossed it, and
were astonished to find that they had become black, except just
those parts of them that had touched the black river, namely,
their mouths, the soles of their feet, and the palms of their
hands. The two who had crossed the black river, however,

were of a pure white colour. The two parties now travelled in different directions, and when they had gone some way, the white men were agreeably surprised to come across a large house containing white wives for them to marry; while the black men also found huts, or shimbees, with black women whom they married. And this is why some people are white and some black.

XXVIII

THE BIRD-MESSENGERS.

ALL the towns in Molembo or Ncotchi were suffering terribly from the awful scourge or evil wind (the disease we know by the name of small-pox). And the chief prince called the princes and people together and asked them if it were not time to ask Nzambi Mpungu why he was so cross with them? And they all agreed that it was so. But whom were they to send? They said that the Ngongongo was a wonderful bird, and could fly in a marvellous way. They sent him with a message to Nzambi Mpungu; but when he got there, and cried out "quang, quang, quang," it was evident that Nzambi Mpungu did not understand his tongue. So he flew back back to Ncotchi and reported his failure.

Then Ncotchi sent the rock-pigeon (mbemba), but he could not make Nzambi Mpungu understand, and he also returned to Ncotchi.

Then the prince sent the ground-dove (ndumbu nkuku), and she went and sang before Nzambi Mpungu:

> " 'Fuka Matenda ma fua
> Vanji Maloango ma fua
> Vanji Makongo ma fua
> Sukela sanga vi sia."

("Mafuka Matenda is dead,
 Vanji Maloango is dead,
 Vanji Makongo is dead ;
 This is the news that I bring."*)

And Nzambi Mpungu heard what the dove had said, but answered not.

* *Mafuka* means *ambassador*, and is a title given to certain rich natives. *Matendu* is the name of a prince of KaCongo. *Vanji* is a title and has the sense of *creator, lord.* The last line is a form expressing that one has delivered one's message.

XXIX.

NZAMBI MPUNGU'S AMBASSADOR.

NZAMBI Mpungu heard that some one across the seas was making people who could speak. This roused his ire, so that he called the ox, the tiger, the antelope, the cock, and other birds together, and after telling them the news, he appointed the cock his ambassador.

"Tell the white man that I alone am allowed to make people who can talk, and that it is wrong of them to make images of men and give them the power of speech."

And the cock left during the night, passing through a village about midnight, and only a few of the people got up to do honour to Nzambi Mpungu's ambassador, so that Nzambi Mpungu waxed wroth, and turned the inhabitants of that village into monkeys.

XXX

WHY THE CROCODILE DOES NOT EAT
THE HEN.

THERE was a certain hen; and she used to go down to the river's edge daily to pick up bits of food. One day a crocodile came near to her and threatened to eat her, and she cried : "Oh, brother, don't!"

And the crocodile was so surprised and troubled by this cry that he went away, thinking how he could be her brother. He returned again to the river another day, fully determined to make a meal of the hen.

But she again cried out : "Oh, brother, don't!"

"Bother the hen!" the crocodile growled, as she once more turned away. "How can I be her brother? She lives in a town on land; I live in mine in the water."

Then the crocodile determined to see Nzambi about the question, and get her to settle it; and so he went his way. He had not gone very far when he met his friend Mbambi (a very large kind of lizard). "Oh, Mbambi!" he said, "I am sorely troubled. A nice fat hen comes daily to the river to feed; and each day, as I am about to catch her, and take her to my home and feed on her, she startles me by calling me 'brother.' I can't stand it any longer; and I am now off to Nzambi, to hold a palaver about it."

"Silly idiot!" said the Mbambi, "do nothing of the sort, or you will only lose the palaver and show your ignorance. Don't you know, dear crocodile, that the duck lives in the water and lays eggs? the turtle does the same; and I also lay eggs. The hen does the same; and so do you, my silly friend. Therefore we are all brothers in a sense." And for this reason the crocodile now does not eat the hen.

XXXI.

THE THREE BROTHERS.

In the beginning, when KaCongo had still one mother, and the whole family yet lived on grass and roots, and knew not how to plant, a woman brought forth three babes at one birth.

"Oh, what am I to do with them?" she cried. "I do not want them; I will leave them here in the grass." And the three little ones were very hungry, and looked about them for food. They walked and walked a long long way, until at last they came to a river, which they crossed.

They saw bananas, and palm-trees, and mandioca, growing in great quantities, but dared not eat the fruit thereof. Then the river-spirit called to them, and told them to eat of these good things. And the tiniest of the three tried a banana and found it very sweet. Then the other two ate them, and found them very good. And after this they ate of the other trees, and so grew up well nurtured and strong; and they learnt how to become carpenters and blacksmiths, and built themselves houses. The river-spirit supplied them with women for wives; and soon they multiplied and created a town of their own.

A man who had wandered far from his town came near to where the three brothers had built their home, and was astonished as he approached it, to hear voices. This man happened to be the father of the three brothers. So he returned to his town, without having entered the village, to tell his wife that he had found her children. Then the old woman set out with her husband to seek for her children, and wandered and wandered on, until she was too tired to go any further, when she sank down by the wayside to rest.

Now one of the children of the three brothers came across the old woman, and was afraid, and ran back to tell his father.

Then the three brothers set out with the intention of killing the intruder ; but the river-spirit called out to them, and told them not to kill her, but to take her to their home, and feed her, for she was their mother. And they did so.

XXXII.

DEATH AND BURIAL OF THE FJORT.

ONE of my cook's many fathers having died (this time, his real father), he came to me with tears in his eyes to ask me for a little rum to take to town, where he said his family were waiting for him. Some days previously the cook had told me that his father was suffering from the sleeping sickness, and was nearing his end, so that when I heard the cry of " Chibai-i " floating across the valley from a little town close to that in which the cook lived, I guessed who the dead one was, and was prepared to lose the cook's services for a certain number of days.

The death of the father of a family is always a very sad event, but the death of the father of a Fjort family seems to me to be peculiarly pathetic. His little village at once assumes a deserted appearance; his wives and sisters, stripped of their gay cloths, wander aimlessly around and about the silent corpse, crying and wringing their hands, their tears coursing down their cheeks along little channels washed in the thick coating of oil and ashes with which they have besmeared their dusky faces. Naked children, bereft for the time being of their mother's care, cry piteously; and the men, with a blue band of cloth (*ntanta mabundi*) tied tightly round their heads, sit apart and in silence, already wondering what evil person or fetish has caused them this overwhelming loss.

The first sharp burst of grief being over, loving hands shave and wash the body, and, if the family be rich enough, palm-wine or rum is used instead of water. Then the heavy body is placed upon mats of rushes and covered with a cloth. After resting in this position for a day, the body is wrapped in long pieces of cloth and placed upon a kind of rack or framework bed, underneath which a hole has been dug to receive the water, etc., that comes from the corpse. A fire is lighted both at the head and foot of the rack, and the body is covered each day with the leaves of the Acaju, so that the smoke that hangs about it will keep off the flies. More cloth is from time to time wrapped around the body; but, unless there are many palavers which cannot be quickly settled, it is generally buried after two or three wrappings. The more important the person, the longer, of course, it takes to settle these palavers and their many complications; and as the body cannot be buried until they are settled, one can understand how the heirs of a great king sometimes come to give up the hope of burying their relation, and leave him unburied for years. On the other hand, the slave, however rich he may be, is quickly buried.

The family being all present, a day is appointed upon which the cause of the death shall be divined. Upon this day the family, and the family in which the deceased was brought up, collect what cloth they can and send it to some well-known Nganga, a long way off. The Nganga meets the messengers and describes to them exactly all the circumstances connected with the life, sickness and death of the deceased; and if they conclude that this information agrees with what they know to be the facts of the case, they place the cloth before him and beseech him to inform them the cause of their relation's death. This the Nganga sets himself to divine.   After some delay he informs the relations (1) that the father has died because some-one (perhaps now dead) knocked a certain nail into a certain fetish, with his death as the end in view, or (2) that so-and-so has bewitched him, or (3) that he died because his time had come.

The relations then go to the Nganga of the fetish or Nkissi mentioned, and ask him if he remembers so-and-so knocking a nail into it? and if so, will he kindly point out the nail to them? He may say Yes. Then they will pay him to draw it out, so that the rest of the family may not die.   Or the relations give the person indicated by the Nganga as having bewitched the dead man, the so-called Ndotchi (witch), a powdered bark, which he must swallow and vomit if he be really innocent.   The bark named *Mbundu* is given to the man who owns to being a witch, but denies having killed the person in question.   That of *Nkassa* is given to those who deny the charge of being witches altogether.   The witches or other persons who, having taken the bark, do not vomit are either killed or die from the effects of the poison, and their bodies used to be burnt.   Since civilized government have occupied the country a slight improvement has taken place, in that the relations of the witch are allowed to bury the body.   If events turns out as divined by the Nganga, he retains the cloth given to him by the relations or their messengers: otherwise he must return it to the family, who take it to another Nganga.

While all this is going on, a carpenter is called in to build the coffin; and he is paid one fowl, one mat of rushes, and one

FUNERAL SHIMBEC.

To face page 113.

closely woven mat per day. Rum and a piece of blue cloth are given to him on the day he covers the case with red cloth. Palm-wine, rum, and cloth are given to him as payment on its completion. And now that all palavers are finished, and the coffin ready, the family are once more called together; and the prince of the land and strangers are invited to come and hear how all the palavers have been settled. A square in front of the shimbec containing the coffin is cleared of herbs and grass, and carefully swept; and here, during the whole night previous to the official meeting, women and children dance. Mats are placed immediately in front of the shimbec for the family and their fetishes (Poomba): the side opposite is prepared for the prince and his followers; and the other two sides are kept for those strangers and guests who care to come. At about three o'clock guns are fired off as a signal that all is ready. The family headed by their elder and spokesman then seat themselves ready to receive their guests. Then the guests glide into the village and make their way to the elder, present themselves, and then take their allotted seats.

When all are assembled, the elder addresses the two family fetishes held by two of the family. Pointing and shaking his hand at them, he tells them how the deceased died, and all the family has done to settle the matter; he tells them how they have allowed the father to be taken, and prays them to protect the rest of the family; and when he has finished his address, the two who hold the fetishes, or wooden figures, pick up a little earth and throw it on the heads of the fetishes, then, lifting them up, rub their heads in the earth in front of them.

Then the elder addresses the prince and his people, and the strangers who have come to hear how the deceased has died, and

I

offers them each a drink.   When they have finished drinking,
he turns to the fetishes and tells them that they have allowed
evil to overtake the deceased, but prays them to protect his
guests from the same.   Then the fetishes again have earth
thrown at them, and their heads are once more rubbed in
the earth.

And now the elder addresses the wives and tells them that
their husband has been cruelly taken from them, and that they
are now free to marry another; and then, turning to the
fetishes, he trusts that they will guard the wives from the evil
that killed their husband; and the fetishes are again dusted and
rubbed in the earth.

On the occasion that I watched these proceedings, the elder
got up and addressed me, telling me that my cook, who had
served me so well and whom I had sent to town when he was
sick, etc., etc., had now lost his father; and once more turning
to his fetishes, the poor creatures were again made to kiss old
mother earth, this time for my benefit.

If a witch has to undergo the bark-test, rum is given to the
prince, and he is told that if he hears that the Ndotchi has been
killed he is to take no official notice of the fact.

Then the men dance all through the night; and the next day
the body is placed in the coffin and buried.   In KaCongo the
coffin is much larger than that made in Loango; and it is placed
upon a huge car on four or six solid wheels.   This car remains
over the grave, ornamented in different ways with stuffed
animals, and empty demijohns, animal-boxes, and other earthenware goods, in accordance with the wealth of the deceased.   I
can remember when slaves and wives were buried together with
the prince; but this custom has now died out in Loango and

PRINCE XIKAIA BY THE FUNERAL CAR OF HIS BROTHER, LINGUISTER FRANCISCO;

Shewing his Uncle's body wrapped in cloth, ready for burial, and remains of the destroyed shimbec of the deceased.

KaCongo, and we only hear of its taking place far away inland.

The " fetish chibinga " * sometimes will not allow the corpse to close its eyes. This is a sure sign that the deceased is annoyed about something, and does not wish to be buried. In such a case no coffin is made, the body is wrapped in mats and placed in the woods near to an Nlomba tree. Should he be buried in the ordinary way, all the family would fall sick and die. Should his chimyumba (KaCongo *chimbindi*) appear to one of his family, that person would surely die. But others not of the family may see it and not die.

The deceased will often not rest quiet until his *nkulu* (soul? spirit?) is placed in the head of one of his relations, so that he can communicate with the family. This is done by the Nganga picking up some of the earth from the grave of the deceased, and, after mixing it with other medicine, placing it in either the horn of an antelope (*lekorla*) or else a little tin box (*nkobbi*). Then seating himself upon a mat within a circle drawn in chalk on the ground, he shakes a little rattle (*nquanga*) at the patient, and goes through some form of incantation, until the patient trembles and cries out with the voice of the deceased, when they all know that the *nkulu* has taken up its residence in his head. The medicine and earth together with the *nkobbi* is called *nkulu mpemba*, and shows that the deceased died of some ordinary disease; but when the medicine and earth are put into the *lekorla* it shows that the deceased died of some sickness of the head, and this is called *nkulu mabiali.*

Chibinga is the state of a corpse which remains with its eyes open, and is also the power, or *nkissi*, that is the cause of this affliction.

The Fjort say the "shadow" ceases at the death of the person. I asked if that was because they kept the corpse in the shade; what if they put the corpse in the sun? The young man asked turned to his elderly aunt and re-asked her this question. "No," she said emphatically, "certainly not!" *

---

* Miss Kingsley writes as follows on this: "The final passage is an unconscious support to my statements regarding the four souls of man. The shadow dies utterly at bodily death; therefore it does not matter whether the corpse is in the sun, or no, because the shadow it might throw would not be the shadow of the man as he was when alive; it would only be the shadow of the dead stuff." (See *Folk-Lore*, vol. viii., p. 144.)

APPENDIX I.

BY MARY H. KINGSLEY.

NZAMBI.

IN the preceding pages Mr. Dennett's observations have been given just as they have reached the hands of the Folk-Lore Society; but there are many more of his observations on the religion of the Fjort which have come into my hands, unfortunately in so scattered a state that they cannot be given as separate chapters, little fragments of a few pages only, paragraphs in letters, and so on. Yet, as these fragments contain much valuable information in themselves, and also help in the understanding of much of the information he has sent home from KaCongo and Loango in a more connected form, I have collected some of them, and give them here without any alteration of Mr. Dennett's words, except obvious and trifling errors.

I have explained in the Introduction that I regard Nkissism as a school of the fetish form of thought, and that I regard Mr. Dennett as the best authority we have on this particular school of this great Nature-Religion. The most important bit of work that he has done for us in the study of Nkissism seems to me to be his explanation of the word Nzambi in its inner meaning. Mr. Dennett himself would probably not agree with me on this point, and prefer to base his claim to honour on his investigation of the inner meaning of the whole Fjort language; but, at present, he has not sent up his observations in this matter in a form that makes sufficient allowance for the ignorance of the civilised world regarding that beautiful but complex form of Bantu; and, as the material Mr. Dennett has sent home regarding the inner meaning of the Fjort language is not printed in this volume, I will confine my collection of supplementary matter to Nzambi and the religion which surrounds her.

Mr. Dennett says in a letter of the 6th July, 1897:

I have translated Nzambi as the Spirit of the Earth or Old Mother Earth. But *Anza* is the River Congo, and so Anzambi might well be translated the River-Spirit; but this does not fit in with Fjorts' explanation of Nzambi, who figures in their folklore as the Great Princess, the mother of all animals, etc., the real truth being that *Anza*, the river, comes out of the earth, *Nsi*. In Fjort legends the river-spirits are legion, the name of the river and the spirit being one, Anzambi then is the spirit of the River Congo. All river-spirits appear to teach some lesson, physical or moral. In one story you will see the river-spirit taught the

Fjort to plant bananas and manioc,* to forge iron and so on; and I have given you the real etymology of the word Nzambi and its real meaning, which fits in with the ideas, with the love of Mother Earth (Nzambi, mother earth) and this knowledge of the Anzambi, River-Spirit.

Nsi the earth may be also translated as the Offspring of the Beginner; then we have the river-spirit of knowledge coming out of the spirit of motherhood, which in its turn is the (N) Offspring of the (isi) Beginner.

That Mr. Dennett is right in this matter I have no doubt from my own investigations of important words in other schools of fetish than Nkissism; but that it will seem clear to those who have not personally wrestled with the difficulties of such words as Nzambi, or Woka, I feel many doubts. I hope, however, Mr. Dennett will soon be able to publish a full account of his long study of the Fjort language, and that may make the affair clearer. Of one thing I am very sure; and that is, that until we know the underlying meaning

* Bananas and manioc were introduced in Fjort culture by the Roman Catholic missionaries, who first landed among the Fjort in 1490, but I found Anyambie as a great god among the Mpongwe, but with them it is not Anyambie, that is connected with knowledge, and with the river, and sea, but Mbuiri (see *Travels in West Africa*, p. 228). The difference between the Fjort and the Mpongwe in this matter is easily explainable, for the Mpongwe did not receive, up any of their rivers, Roman Catholic missionaries to the same extent and in the same manner as the Fjorts received, *viâ* the Congo, instruction and new articles of food. The underlying idea, which is earlier than the introduction of manioc and bananas, is identical. M. H. K.

of the languages of Africa, we cannot safely dog-
matise regarding the African's religion.   I do not
say that when Mr. Dennett does publish his key to
the Fjort alphabet, he and I will be found to agree
in all deductions ; because, although we both steep
our minds in black and agree in black, we, in our
white capacities, start from very different points of
view in these matters.

I now pass on to another fragment of Mr. Dennett's
observations on Nzambi, wherein he says:

ABOUT NZAMBI.

It is the most difficult thing in the world at present, I think,
to get a clear definition of Nzambi Mpungu, or of Nzambi, from
the natives themselves in a direct way.

Some say that Nzambi Mpungu made the world and sent
Nzambi there, and that then he came down and married his
creation, and thus became the father of us all.   And of course
we have distorted versions of the Creation according to the
Bible.   God, we are told, made man and woman, and put them
in a large white house in a beautiful garden and told them not
to eat of the tree of shame.   But before they took charge of their
house, thousands and thousands of rats trooped out of it.   They
ate of the tree of shame, and when God called to see them they
were ashamed and dared not come out.   And so forth.

Still the faint notion of a spirit that rules the rains and sends
the lightning, and gives them rainbows, exists ; and they call
that very humanised spirit Nzambi Mpungu.

CLIMBING A PALM-TREE FOR PALM-WINE.

To face page 121.

But Nzambi, as the great princess that governed all on earth, is ever in their mouths as a mighty ruler, and she seems to have obtained the spirit of rain, lightning, etc., and to have buried it in her bowels. The following is a little story that gives her a human shape, and fixes her position as a mother:

Some women were busy planting in a country where water was scarce, so that they had brought their sangas, containing that precious fluid, with them. As they were working, a poor old woman, carrying a child on her back, passed by them, hesitated for a moment, and then walked back to them and asked them to give her child a cup of water.

The women said that they had carried the water from afar, and needed it for themselves, as there was no water just there.

The poor old woman passed on, but told them that they would one day regret their want of charity.

Noticing a man up a palm tree, she asked him if he would mind giving her baby a little palm-wine, as the poor little thing, she was afraid, was dying of thirst.

" Why not, mother?" he replied, and straightway came down the tree and placed a calabash at her feet.

" But I have no cup," she said.

" Nay, mother, let me break this spare calabash, and give the child a drink."

She thanked him, and went her way, saying : " Be here, my son, at this time to-morrow."

He wondered what the old woman meant ; but such was the impression her words had made upon him, that he could not sleep at all that night, and felt himself obliged, when the morrow came, to proceed to the place.

" Surely this cannot be the place," he said, as he came near
to the palm-tree where he had met the old woman. "There was
no water where the women were at work yesterday, yet surely
that is a great lake."

"Wonder not, my son," said the old woman, as she approached
him, " for thus have I punished the women for their want of
charity. See my son, this lake is full of fish, and you and all
men may fish here daily, and the abundance of fish shall never
grow less. But no woman shall eat the fish thereof, for as sure
as she eats the fish of this lake, so surely shall she immediately
die. Let the lake and its fish be *kazila* for women. For I,
Nzambi, have so ordered it." Nzambi then loaded the young
man with many gifts, and told him to depart in peace. The
name of this lake is Bòsi, and it is situated a few miles inland
behind a place called Futilla.

Another story proves to us that retribution is an attribute of
Nzambi:

An old lady, after some days' journey, arrived at a town called
Sonanzenzi, footsore and weary, and covered with those terrible
sores that afflict a great number of the Negroes in the Congo
district. The old lady asked for hospitality from each house-
holder as she passed through the town; but they all refused to
receive her, saying that she was unclean, until she arrived at the
very last house. Here the kind folk took her in, nursed and
cured her. When she was quite well and about to depart, she
told her kind friends to pack up their traps and leave the town
with her, as assuredly it was accursed and would be destroyed
by Nzambi. And the night after they had left it, heavy rains
fell, and the town was submerged, and all the people drowned,
for Sonanzenzi was in a deep valley, quite surrounded by hills.

And now as the people of Tandu pass on their way to Mbuela, and they look down into the deep waters, they notice the sticks of the houses at the bottom ; and they remember that Nzambi would have them take care of the sick, and not turn them cruelly away from their doors.

From the following, one gathers that Nzambi is also a judge :

Nzambi was in her town resting, when she was called to settle a palaver in a town close to.　She and her followers went, and after the usual preliminary formalities, commenced to talk the palaver.　While they were yet talking, Nzambi heard the drum beaten in her own town, and wondered greatly what the matter could be.　She sent the pig to see what the disturbance was, and to find out who had dared to beat her Ndungu zilo, or great drum, during her absence. But the pig returned, and said: " Princess, I did not see anyone in the town, and all was quiet and in order."

" Strange ! " said Nzambi, "but I distinctly heard the beating of my drum."

They continued the palaver until Nzambi again heard her drum beating.

"Go immediately, O antelope ! " said Nzambi, " and find out who is beating my drum."

The antelope went and returned; but he had not seen nor heard anything.　They continued the palaver, and just as they drew it to a close, Nzambi heard the drum a third time.

" Let us all go and find out," said Nzambi, " who has thus dared to disturb us."

They went, but saw nothing.

" Hide yourselves in the grass round about the town, and watch for the intruder ! "

Then they saw the crab coming out of the water. Breathlessly they all watched him. They saw the crab creep stealthily up to the drum and beat it. Then they heard him sing:

" Oh, Nzambi has gone up to the top of the mountain, and left me here all alone."

Then the people rushed out of the grass, and caught the terrified crab and dragged him to Nzambi.

And Nzambi rebuked him saying : " Thou hast acted as one without a head, henceforth thou shall be headless, and shalt be eaten by all men."

According to another crab story, Nzambi had already given the crab a body and legs, and promised on the next day to give him a head. Then the crab sent invitations to all around to come and see Nzambi place his head on. And when they had all arrived, he was so proud that he could hardly walk straight. But Nzambi rebuked him for his great pride, and told those who were present that as a warning to them not to be self-glorious she would not give the crab a head. And thus it happens that when the crab wants to see where he is going, he has to lift his eyes out of his body.

Nzambi Mpungu made the world and all the people in it. But Nzambi had made no drum for her people, so that they could not dance. Nchonzo nkila, a little bird with a long tail, fashioned like a native drum that seems always to be beating the earth, lived in a small village near to the town that Nzambi had chosen as her place of residence. This Nchonzo nkila set to work, and was the first to make a drum. He then called his followers together, and they beat the drum and danced. And when Nzambi heard the beating of the drum she wanted it, so that her people might also dance. " What ! " she said to her people, " I, a great princess, cannot dance, because I have no drum, while that little wagtail dances to the beat of the drum he has made. Go now, O antelope, and tell the little wagtail that his Great Mother wants his drum."

And the antelope went to wagtail's town and asked him to send Nzambi his drum.

" Nay," answered the wagtail, " I cannot give Nzambi my drum, because I want it myself."

" But," said the antelope, " the great mother gave you your life ; surely you owe her something in return."

" Yes, truly," answered wagtail, " but I cannot give her my drum."

" Lend it to me then," said the antelope, " that I may play it for you."

" Certainly," said the wagtail.

But after beating the drum for a short time, the antelope ran away with it. Then wagtail waxed exceeding wrath, and sent his people after him. And they caught the antelope and killed him, and gave him to their women to cook for them.

After a while Kivunga, the hyena, was sent by Nzambi to see why the antelope was so long away. And he asked Nchonzo nkila what had become of the antelope. And Nchonzo nkila told him.

" Give me then some of his blood, that I may take it to our mother, and show her."

Nchonzo nkila gave him some, and Kivunga took it to Nzambi, and told her all that had occurred. And Nzambi was grieved at not being able to secure the drum. Then she addressed the Mpacasa, or wild ox, and besought him to get her the drum. But Mpacasa tried the same game as the antelope, and met

with the same fate. Kivunga came again, and was told by the
wagtail that Mpacasa had been killed by his people for trying
to steal the drum. Kivunga returned to Nzambi, and told her
how Mpacasa had tried to run away with the drum, and had
been killed. Nzambi grieved sorely, and would not be com-
forted, and cried out to her people, praying them to get her
Nchonzo nkila's drum.

Then Mfiti (the ant) stood out from among the people and
volunteered, saying: "Weep not, O Nzambi, I will get the
drum for you."

"But you are so small a creature, how will you secure the
drum?"

"From the fact of my being so small I shall escape
detection."

And so the ant went out to wagtail's town, and waited
there until all were asleep. Then he entered the house where
the drum was kept, and carried it away unperceived, and
brought it to Nzambi. And Nzambi rewarded the ant and
then beat the drum and made all her people dance.

Then Nchonzo nkila heard the noise, and said: "Listen!
they are dancing in Nzambi's town. Surely they have stolen
my drum."

And when they looked in the house for the drum, they found
it not. So Nchonzo nkila became very angry and called all the
birds together; and they all came to hear what he had to say,
save the Mbemba, or pigeon. Then they discussed the matter
and decided upon sending Nzambi a messenger, asking her to
appoint a place of meeting where the palaver between them
might be talked. And Nzambi promised to be in Neamlau's
town the next day to talk the palaver over before that prince.

Then Nchonzo nkila and his followers went to Neamlau's town and awaited Nzambi. Two days they waited, and on the third Nzambi and her people arrived.

Then Nchonzo nkila said : " O, prince ! I made a drum and Nzambi has taken it from me. It is for her to tell you why ; let her speak."

Nzambi arose and said : " O, prince ! My people wished to dance, but we had no drum, and therefore they could not. Now I heard the sound of a drum being beaten in the village over which I had set Nchonzo nkila to rule. I therefore first sent the antelope as my ambassador to Nchonzo nkila, to ask him for the drum ; but his people killed the antelope. I then sent Mpacasa for the drum ; but they killed him also, as Kivunga will bear witness. Finally I sent the ant; and he brought me the drum, and my people danced and we were happy. Surely, O prince, I who brought forth all the living in this world have a right to this drum if I want it."

Then Kivunga told them all he knew of the palaver.

Nenlau* and his old men, having heard all that was said, retired to drink water. When he returned, Nenlau said : " You have asked me to decide this question, and my judgment is this : It is true that Nzambi is the mother of us all, but Nchonzo nkila certainly made the drum. Now when Nzambi made us, she left us free to live as we chose, and she did not give us drums at our birth. The drums we make ourselves ; and they are therefore ours, just as we may be said to be Nzambi's. If she had made drums and sent them into the world with us, then the drums would be hers. But she did

---

Nenlau is a contracted form of Neamlau.

not. Therefore she was wrong to take the drum from Nchonzo nkila."

Nzambi paid Nchonzo nkila for the drum, and was fined for the mistake.

Then both Nzambi and Nchonzo nkila gave presents to Nenlau and went their way.

Thus, in this case, we have Nzambi brought down to the level of the rest of the world, and judged by human laws. And such is the native idea of their second divinity; for while they willingly give her credit for being the mother of all things and full of all power, they cannot entertain the idea of her being other than human.

NZAMBI'S DAUGHTER AND HER SLAVE.

Nzambi had a most beautiful daughter, and she took the greatest care of her. As the child grew up, she was kept within the house, and never allowed to go outside, her mother alone waiting upon her. And when she arrived at the age of puberty, her mother determined to send her to a town a long way off, that she might be undisturbed while she underwent her purification in the paint-house.

She gave her child a slave; and unnoticed these two left Nzambi's town for the distant place where the paint-house was situated.

" Oh, see there, slave ! what is that ? "

" Give me your anklets, and I will tell you," answered the slave.

The daughter of Nzambi gave the slave the anklets.

"That is a snake."

And then they walked along for some time, when suddenly the daughter of Nzambi said: "Oh, slave, what is that?"

"Give me your two new cloths, and I will tell you."

She gave the slave the two cloths.

"That is an antelope."

They had not gone far when the daughter again noticed something strange.

"Slave, tell me what that thing is?"

"Give me your bracelets."

The girl gave the slave her bracelets.

"That thing is an eagle."

The princess thought it wonderful that the slave should know so much more than she did; and when she caught sight of a thing rising gently from the ground, she turned to her again and asked: "And what is that?"

"Give me your coral necklace."

The girl gave the slave the coral.

"That is a butterfly."

The next time she asked the slave for information, the slave made her change her clothes with her; so that while she was nearly naked, the slave was dressed most beautifully. And in this fashion they arrived at their destination, and delivered their message to the prince.

After the proper preparations they placed the slave in the paint-house, with all the ceremony due to a princess; and they set the daughter of Nzambi to mind the plantations. In her innocence and ignorance the daughter of Nzambi at first thought all this was in order, and part of what she had to go

K

through ; but in a very short time she began to realize her position, and to grieve about it.   She used to sing plaintive songs as she minded the corn, of how she had been mistaken for a slave, while her slave was honoured as a princess.   And the people thought her mad.   But one day a trade-caravan passed her and she asked the trader where he was going, and he answered : " To Nzambi's town."

" Will you then take a message to Nzambi for me."

The trader gladly assented.

" Then tell her that her daughter is as a slave watching the plantations, while the slave is in the paint-house."

He repeated the message ; and when she had said that it was correct, he went on his way and delivered it to Nzambi.

Nzambi and her husband immediately set out in their hammock, accompanied by many followers, for the town where she had sent her daughter.   And when she arrived she was greatly shocked to see her daughter in that mean position, and would have punished the prince, had she not seen that he and his people were not to blame.

They called upon the slave to come out of the paint-house. But she was afraid, and would not.   Then they entered, and having stripped her of all her borrowed plumes, they shut her within the house and burnt her.

Mr. Dennett also informs me that, in districts occupied by Fjort south of the Congo, the high roads from the sea to the capital town are called " the footsteps of Nzambi."   We now pass on to the consideration of

the cult which has Nzambi for its central object,
namely the cult of Nkissism.   Mr. Dennett says:

NKISSISM.

Nkissi means the mysterious power that is contained in plants
and herbs and earth, or, as we should say, the medicine or poison.
Hence it comes to mean any mysterious power—in short, a
mystery.   The power of the hypnotiser is called Nkissi; the
hypnotiser is called Ndotchi or Ndokki.   The poisoner is also
called by this name.   To explain the Great Something, the
unknown power that certainly governs the universe, has puzzled
the Fjort, as it has puzzled all others who have tried to dive
beyond the regions of certainty.   But while others have reasoned
and sought after wisdom, Fjort has just put the whole matter
on one side, and called it Nkissi.   So that it has not been a
search after wisdom so much as a severe letting alone.   His
knowledge has come to him from his experience of a series of
hard lessons in every-day life.

He suffered pain; fire burnt him; water drowned him;
without food he hungered; sickness caused him pain, and death
followed sickness.   He ascribed it to Nkissi.   Herbs poisoned
some people, and herbs contained the power that cured others—
Nkissi.   Here there was something visible that contained the
Nkissi; that caused pain and relieved it.   Whence this power?
It grew with the trees and herbs out of the earth: Nkissi
nsi, the mysterious power that comes from the earth.   Fearful
earth, or Nza-mbi, really, terrible firstborn, mother, or producer.   The earth is the father's firstborn; the father's name,
Mpungu.

Thus have we arrived at the name the Fjort has given to the Creator. He calls him Nzambi Mpungu, the Father of the Fearful Firstborn, or Earth.

The Rev. Père Alexandre Visseq, in his *Fiot Dictionary*, under the heading " Nzambi," says it means " God, the Supreme Being, Creator and Preserver of the Universe. The Negroes believe in a Supreme Being who has made all things. According to them, he is a great monarch who has a great number of wives and beautiful children. He passes a happy existence in the heavens, and scarcely troubles himself about us. As he is not wicked, there is no use in their offering him sacrifices. Below him there are smaller divinities capable of doing harm. It is necessary to pray to them, invoke them and adore them. God is not jealous of the worship people render to them," and so on. I think we need not pursue this definition any further. There can be no doubt that the Supreme Being, Nzambi Mpungu, and Nzambi, Mother Earth, are two separate and distinct conceptions.

But we have another dictionary to appeal to, that of Mr. Bentley, a Baptist missionary in the Congo. And his vast knowledge of the natives and their language commands our respect. He writes: " The root of the word Nzambi has not been found in Congo. It is suggested by Mr. Kobbe in his Huero Dictionary that in Kurunga, ' Ndyambi ' = God, and Ndyambi is derived from Yamba, to present on a special occasion, and connects it with Ndyembi, a reward, to which may be allied the Congo Nzamba, a toll for a bridge or a ferry. These suggestions can scarcely be regarded as satisfactory." So much for this authority.

But in the Tandu dialect of the Congo district, the word

Mpungu means Father in the sense of Creator. And in the words: Nsusu, the young of a fowl, chicken; Nswa, the child; Nsa, dependents; Nsa Ka, the title of the heir apparent of the throne of Congo; we have a root which, in each case, refers to immediate offspring or dependence.

You will also learn as we proceed that Nzambi is talked of as the mother of all things, the first daughter of the first father. Nza, the earth, was the creator's first creation. That the earth that contained the Nkissi that poisoned or cured people should have been called the bad (mbi) earth, in the sense of the earth that is to be feared, is surely not a wonderful conclusion.

Hence Nza mbi, I conclude, first meant the Fearful First-born and producer. Thus we have Nkiss nsi, Nzambi's spirit, mystery in the earth; Nzambi, the Fearful First-born of Mpungu, the Father: a Trinity.

Mpungu, or, as he is more often called, Nzambi Mpungu, the father of the Fearful First born, is seldom invoked by the natives. He is far above them. A father perhaps; but do not the children belong to the mother? and is it not to their mother and her family that they must look for assistance? The line between the white man's God and Nzambi Mpungu is a very thin one. The Negro has got as far as natural religion will take him, and admits that he knows little or nothing about Him. He is willing to believe whatever the white man likes to tell him. And thus we have Nzambi Mpungu, the father of Nzambi, described to us in their mythology, or folklore, as a human being—as a naked man. This idea has crept into their minds through their having come across pictures of Our Lord as he is painted dying for us upon the cross.

There is a man still living who declares that he was translated to heaven and saw Nzambi Mpungu. He lives in a town not far from Loango. He says that one day, when it was thundering and lightning and raining very heavily, and when all the people in his village, being afraid, had hidden themselves in their shimbecs, he alone was walking about. Suddenly, and at the moment of an extraordinarily vivid flash of lightning, after a very loud peal of thunder, he was seized and carried through space until he reached the roof of heaven, when it opened and allowed him to pass into the abode of Nzambi Mpungu. Nzambi Mpungu cooked some food for him, and gave him to eat. And when he had eaten, he took him about and showed him his great plantations and rivers full of fish, and then left him, telling him to help himself whenever he felt hungry. He stayed there two or three weeks, and never had he had such an abundance of food. Then Nzambi Mpungu came to him again, and asked him whether he would like to remain there always, or whether he would like to return to the earth. He said that he missed his friends, and would like to return to them. Then Nzambi Mpungu sent him back to his family.*

I have said in the Introduction, that from historical tradition and from internal evidence, it is clear that Nkissism is a superimposed religion on the peoples of Loango and KaCongo, and that I believe the religion that was extant in these regions before the coming of the sons of the king of Congo and the priests of the Congo religion (Nkissism) was a religion identical

---

* This story was told to me by Antonio Lavadeiro, my linguister, or head-man, at Bintamba, River Chiloango.

in essentials with that which I had opportunities of studying among the tribes of the Mpongwe stem (Mpongwe, Ajumba, Orungu, Nkâmi and Igalwa); and I may remark that among these tribes there is not a priesthood apart, but the house-father is the priest of his people. The following observations of Mr. Dennett seem to me to have a bearing on this point.

NKISSINSI.

And now it is that we come to Nkissi, the spirit, the power, the mystery, that is contained in the Bilongo, or medicines, in the earth, and trees, and herbs.

The father of the tribe carefully guarded one spot within his domain, in which he planted a stunted baobab, or placed a sacred stone, or a wooden image. Nails were not driven into this image, and the place so set apart was sacred—sacred to the mysterious power or spirit—and this was called his Nkissinsi. He was father and priest, or Nganga, the man learned in the folklore of his people. He it was who cured the sick, and instructed the young by his wise words and stories. He, as the direct descendant of Nzambi, ruled his people by that moral authority that devolved from what he considered his God.

But as this family became great, it was ruled not only by the father, but by those elders that he might select to govern certain districts under him; and these lieutenants in their turn appointed others to govern small portions of their regency. And finally Ngangas, or priests, men learned in folklore and medicine, were sent to help these lieutenants, and thus the office of ruler and

priest, the effective authority and the moral authority, were
separated, although the elder still considered himself as high-priest
and ruler.   The Ngangas became a class apart under the title of
Zinganga Nkissi (Zinganga being the plural of Nganga).

These Zinganga developed Nkissism as time went on, and
instituted the Nkissi, or wooden image of a man or a beast
charged with medicines.   The petitioner who wished to kill the
thief who had stolen some of his property, made the Nganga
an offering, and drove a nail into the image as he made his
request.   Or the friends of the sick man would present their
offering to the Nganga of a certain Nkissi ; and he would present
them with some bracelet or amulet, Nkissi, charged with medicine which he affirmed would certainly cure the sick man.

What a field was thus opened to unscrupulous Ngangas, and
how quick they were to avail themselves of their chance, we can
easily realise.

The Zinganga at last professed to be able to call down the
rain from heaven, and thus held the whole country in fear and
trembling while they filled their pockets with their peace
offerings ; and they backed up their profession by wholesale
murder and poisoning of all unbelievers.   They hypnotised the
weak, who thought that some evil Nkissi had possession of them,
until the patient's friends paid the Zinganga heavily to come and
cast out the evil spirit, or killed them as so-called witches.
They usurped the powers of the Elders, and cast off their
allegiance to their great Father, until the great kingdom of
the Bantu became cut up into innumerable petty sovereignties.

The month of February is sacred to Nkissinsi.   This month
is called Muauda.   The prince calls all his people before him and
addresses them ; they then clean the holy ground of all grass

and herbs, and for the first fifteen days the people dance and sing. On the fifteenth day all fetishes (Nkissi) are covered up, and no one is allowed to touch an image until the new moon appears again.

The day of the week upon which the prince calls his people together to discuss any subject is called Nduka. Palavers concerning dead people are talked over on the day called Ntono.

The Fjort has four days in his week: Tono; Silu; Nkandu; Nsona, the fourth day, upon which the women will not work in the fields, sacred to production and motherhood.

Touching those things which the Fjort regard as forbidden, and which they call Xina (thina, or tchina), the youngest resident amongst them must have noticed many of these Xina Swine, which no prince will touch. In addition to these, the Fjort regard all things that come from the sea and have not fins and scales as forbidden, and also all eagles, crows, cuckoos, hawks, owls, herons, bats, and snakes.

So long as he knows nothing about it he says he may eat food out of unclean pots, but if he knows that anything unclean has been cooked in the pot in which his food has been prepared, and he eats thereof, he will be punished by some great sickness coming over him, or by death.

The rites of purification are numerous. After menstruation, childbirth, or sickness, they anoint their bodies with palm-oil mixed with the red powder called takula.

Lastly, I give a note of Mr. Dennett's on the Nkissi of the Musurongo. These Musurongo to this day keep up their tradition for turbulence and miscellaneous villainy with which the Roman Catholic missionaries

of the 15th and 16th centuries credited them. They
are the descendants of the people of " the Count of
Sogno." I also venture to think that they are a
people upon whom Nkissism is a superimposed
religion; but the superimposition of this religion
on the Musurongo took place prior to superimposition of it on the people of Loango and KaCongo.
We have, however, no white record on this point, but
it shows faintly here and there in the black tradition,
the Musurongo being frequently called " the bastard
tribe, or people," and so on. Nevertheless, the information Mr. Dennett gives of these Nkissi at the present day is of such interest that I include it here.

The principal Nkissi, or wooden images, into which nails are
driven in this part of the Musurongo territory are:

Kabata, which is said to kill its victims by giving them the
sleeping sickness.

Nsimbi, that causes dropsy.

Quansi, that infests them with a ceaseless itching.

Then we have their rain-giver, or withholder, called Nvemba.

The Nkissist is robbed, and straightway he goes to the Nganga
of Kabata, with an offering, and knocks a nail into the Nkissi
(or fetish, as you are given to calling it) that the robber may be
plagued with the sleeping sickness and die.

Has he the sleeping sickness, the Nkissist goes to the Nganga,
and, perhaps, confesses his sin, and pays him to withdraw the
nail and cure him.

It has not rained as it should have done; then the prince collects cloth and goods from his people to present to the Nganga Nvemba; and they all go to the sacred grove, and having made their offering sing and dance, and clap their hands and shout for rain. The Nganga secures them this blessing if he can; but if he cannot, it is because someone has committed some great act of indecency, or has broken some of the orders of Nvemba—perhaps someone has been digging up the gum copal and selling it to some trader. The fault at any rate is never with the Nganga; and some victim or other is pounced upon and has to appease the wrathful Nvemba by either losing his life, or that of a slave, or else by paying the Nganga.

But if the thief or sinner who has kindled the wrath of Nvemba will not confess his fault, how then is the culprit to be brought to justice?

The Nganga Nkissi is not behind the sainted priests of our own church in its infancy, and is privileged to proceed by the ordeal of poison, fire, and water. And this again opens to the unscrupulous Nganga a wide field for what is called priestly jugglery, although I do not believe that the Ngangas, who in their simplicity appeal to the interposition of the Great Hidden Power, are necessarily impostors; for they certainly are not.

What we will call the conscience, for want of a better word, of people such as these KaCongos, who are still under the power of a religion full of superstition, is peculiarly sensitive. As then they fully believe that the Great Hidden Power will expose them, is it a wonderful conclusion to arrive at that this fear reacts upon their system? The next time you are in fear and trembling, just try to eat a mouthful of dry bread; and I think that after that you will be a step nearer faith in trial by ordeal than you are to-day, and that you will easily understand how a native suffering from a guilty conscience, and dreading discovery, standing in the presence of the Nganga and the people, when suddenly called upon to swallow a piece of dry mandioco, may probably be choked in his terrible effort to do so. And if fear acts upon the system in this way in this case, why should we doubt its action in other ordeals?

The swindling comes in when a rich sinner confesses his sin to the Nganga, and bribes him to see him through the ordeal safely. The Nganga promises; and the sinner, no longer the victim of fear, gets through the ordeal, even if the Nganga does not help him. But the unscrupulous Nganga does often help by putting a bean in the powdered bark, or casca, and thus ensuring its rejection by the stomach, and by other tricks known to him.

We know that St. Wilfrid built an abbey near Ripon, which was destroyed by fire in 950, and that the privilege of ordeal by fire and water was granted to this church; yet we do not hear people talking of St. Wilfrid as an old humbug. They give him the benefit of the doubt, and call him a saint. And yet I have no doubt that there were unscrupulous priests in those days, quite equal in villany to the vilest Nganga Nkissi of to-day.

But before a man is brought to his trial there must be some evidence against him; and this is supplied by the Nganga, who, having gone through a process of divining, accuses the man of being a poisoner, spell-binder, thief, or adulterer. Thus, a person falling sick will not presume that his sickness is brought about by his own folly, but rather concludes that someone is quietly poisoning him. He therefore calls in a Nganga; and it

is this man's business to divine the evil-doer, or to tell the
sufferer that his sickness is a natural one.

I have often known my servants get up in the night after a
disagreeable dream and fire off their guns to drive the evil
power away, and the next day busy themselves by divining who
the person was that was trying to get at them.

I will close this collection of miscellaneous fragments with an account Mr. Dennett gives of the
method of conducting a native palaver, a story that
shows in what respect the decisions of the law were
held, and a story showing the danger that is in
words.

PALAVERS.

It has struck me, as it must have struck all residents in Africa,
that the force of reason and logic, as illustrated in his many
palavers, plays no mean part in the life of the Fjort.

A discussion takes place between two natives which leads to a
quarrel. Each party relates his side of the question to some
friend, these friends enter into the discussion, but fail to settle
the question in dispute. A bet is then made between the two
in the following way : one offers the other a corner of his cloth
(a dress), and the other taking his knife cuts it off. Or a stick is
broken into two parts, each keeping his part until the palaver is
settled. The dispute is then referred to a prince, in whose presence it is "talked out." This prince decides the matter, and is
paid for his trouble. This the Fjort calls "Ku funda nKana,"
that is to plead and circumstantiate a cause.

Palavers of the above kind of course are easily settled, but the

more serious questions, such as those of shedding blood and inter-
tribal dispute, are far more imposing and formal. It matters
not whether the tribes have had recourse to arms in their en-
deavours to settle the palaver; no question is considered finally
settled until it has been properly and judicially talked out. In
wars of this kind the stronger may gain the day, but the
weaker, if not entirely annihilated, will bide his time, and bring
the palaver up again on some future and more favourable occasion, and probably be successful in getting right given to him
after all. The palaver settled, the fine inflicted paid, the whole
question is closed for ever.[*]

The princes before whom the palaver is to be talked are
generally seated near the trunk of some wide-spreading, shade-
giving tree. The audience sit opposite to them—the defendant
and plaintiff and their followers on either side, the space left
being thus formed with a hollow square.

If the palaver is one of great importance, and the parties
opposed to each other are wealthy, they will employ their
pleaders or Nzonzi (who know how to speak). The plaintiff
states his case. The defendant states his. The simple hearing
of the supposed facts of the case may take days, for each has to
trace back the palaver to its origin. " If you want to catch a
rat," says the Fjort, " go to its hole." Then the Nzonzi of the
plaintiff argues the case, showing that under each head his
party is in the right, illustrating his speech by well-known
comparisons, proverbs, truisms, and songs. The Nzonzi of
the defendant, on the other hand, takes up each heading and
argues against it. The followers on each side emphasize each

---

[*] This is common to all the West African tribes I know, and not confined to the Fjort. M. H. K.

conclusion drawn by the Nzonzi by repeating his last sentence, by clapping their hands, or by joining in the chorus of the song that the Nzonzi has sung to illustrate his case. If this song is a stirring one and does not tell much either way, princes and audience as well as both sides join in it until by a terrific grunt the presiding prince silences the court.

This kind of thing goes on for many days, perhaps, until the two have as it were talked themselves dry, then, after leaving the court to drink water (as they say), the princes, having decided upon the guilt of the litigant, return. The presiding prince then, going through the counts once more, gives his judgment. Song after song is sung, hands are clapped, and telling words are repeated, until as the prince nears the end of his discourse the whole court is led by pure reason to admit the justice of his words and judgment.

Then a great uproar ensues, the last song is sung with terrible enthusiasm, men jump up and twist themselves about, dancing and waving their spears and guns above their heads. The condemned is fined and given so many days to pay, or if the punishment be death, he is immediately tied up and either killed or ransomed according to his position. If the dispute has been between two tribes, after the fine has been paid an agreement is made between the two parties, and a slave killed, to seal the compact.

THE STORY OF A PARTNERSHIP.

There were two partners in trade, but they were of different tribes; one was of the tribe of Mandamba, the other of that of Nsasso. They were going to sell a goat. On their way to market the Mandamba man said to the Nsasso man : " You go on ahead, while I go into the bush ; I will tie the goat up here, and catch you up shortly."

" Ah," thought the Nsasso man, " he wants to give me the slip."

So he assented and went on ahead. But when he saw that the Mandamba man had tied up the goat and gone into the bush, he came back and took the goat, and sold it quickly. Then he returned to the Mandamba man. They met, and the Nsasso man asked the Mandamba man how it was that he had been so long.

" Oh, I have lost the goat," he replied.

" Well, how stupid it was of you not to have given me charge of the goat while you went into the bush ! "

" Let us go to the market," said the Mandamba man, " we may find the goat there " (for a suspicion of what had occurred crossed his mind).

" Very well," said the Nsasso man.

On arriving at the market they saw the goat in the hands of a certain man.

" Who sold you that goat ? " said the Nsasso man.

" Why, you to be sure," said the man.

" In truth then our partnership is at an end, for you have grossly deceived me," said the Mandamba man.

And they went before the king, Ntoka Matunga, and the Nsasso man said he thought the Mandamba man meant to play him a trick.

" Yes," said the king, " perhaps he did intend to do so, as you are of different families, and do not trust one another ; but you did play the trick, which amounts to robbery." The king

condemned the Nsasso man to be burnt, but he promised to pay
the price of his life to the Mandamba man, and the latter agreed
to receive payment, and thus the palaver was settled.

THE DANGER IN WORDS.

The Fjort, as we have seen, is quick to give a subtle meaning
to words that may have no evil significance. The following may
help to bring this force of words before you.

Kingolla one day went to Banana and came back to his town
in rather a happy state, and thus influenced he called upon his
sister Cha and said : " Keep up your health and strength and
look well after your children, they are of a great family, and
must live to prolong the race."

" What can he mean ? " thought the sister. " We are all in
good health ! "

Next day one of the children fell sick and died. And Cha
told her father all that Kingolla had said, and how she feared
that he had bewitched her little one.

The father accused Kingolla of having poisoned the little
one.

Kingolla denied the charge.

" Take casca * then," said the father, " and let God judge
between us."

Kingolla took casca and vomited, thus proving his innocence.

I watched Kingolla's career, and as it may interest you
to know more about him, I give you the following as a sequel
to the above.

Some time after this, Kingolla committed adultery with the
wife of a man named Lallu. Lallu caught him in the act,

* Casca, or cassia, or NKasa, the powdered bark of a tree.

and fell upon his wife, and stabbed her to death. Then the father of the woman was very wroth with Lallu for spilling the blood of his daughter, when by the laws of the land he (the father) was willing to take his daughter back again and to pay Lallu, not only what he had received for her, but also a sum equal to the value of the food and clothing Lallu had given her during the time she had been with him. Thus the father declared war against Lallu and his family, and they fought. Now Kingolla joined the side of the father, and was the only man killed in that war.

Since the foregoing was in type I have received Mr. Dennett's notes on certain points raised in the Introduction. Such of them as relate to Nkissism and the allied subject of Kazila, or Xina, are here inserted, at the risk of some repetition, since they help us to form a clearer conception of those matters.

Nkissism is divided into four parts : 1. Nkissi'nsi (or Nkissi anci) Earth or Nature ; Nkissi, with the king as high priest. 2. Nkissi, the wooden images into which nails are driven, with their priests or Ngangas. This division may be termed Nganga Nkissi. 3. Nkissi kissi, little fetishes, or family fetishes, with a family Nganga. 4. Medicines, with their Nganga bilongo, or medicine man.

The division here made by Mr. Dennett is interesting, because, under the four fairly distinct schools of

Fetish existent in West Africa, you will find these four divisions in the religion. I would prefer to use the word *departments*, for the form of religion each of these departments deals with is the same in essence. The king deals with one class of affairs, the medicine-man with another, and the private individual sees to his home-fetish for himself. Mr. Dennett has called the Nganga bilongo " the medicine-man," but this term, I think, belongs more correctly to the Nganga Nkissi. For the Nganga bilongo is the Fjort representative of our apothecary, and is quite a reasonable person in his way, and it is Nganga Nkissi who represents that class to which the name " medicine-man " has been applied by European writers. Nganga in Fjort, Mr. Dennett says, means Repeater, *i.e.* he who repeats the secrets of native religion, family affairs, or medicine, or, as I should say, those parts of religion appertaining to these several things; for no Nganga tackles all of them, but takes a department.

Mr. Dennett's most important statement is on Kazila, he says:

As it is pronounced to-day it might mean " no road," and we must remember that in old Portuguese *ch* had the force of *k*, and *g* had a sound between *j* and *z*. So Merolla's " Chegilla " is evidently the same thing as the Kăzila. But there is something uncanny about this word; for some natives say it was given them by the Portuguese, and if so, *ka* or *ke* is simply a prefix, and the word was *gira*, which means *gibberish* or *cant*. The Fjort cannot roll his *r* or put *l* in its place.

The native word (about which there is no doubt) for these things forbidden is (s.) *xina* (for) *Bina*. It is xina to steal, to murder, to sleep with a woman on the bare earth, and to eat a certain number of food-stuffs. The punishment is not always death. Sometimes the punishment for eating a forbidden food shows itself in the culprit's coming out in spots and blotches. I know one family that will not eat pigeons, because that bird, by scratching, let light into a cave in which one of the family's ancestors had been made a prisoner. Death is certainly not necessarily the punishment for breaking one's xina.

Merolla's tale, which Miss Kingsley quotes in the Introduction (p. xxv.), proves that so long as the young Negro knew nothing about it, he was "as right as a trivet," and that it was only when he was roughly told the truth that his fear and power of imagination got the better of him and killed him. That tale is incomplete, for, according to native law, the host was the cause of the young Negro's death, and it should end up with : " and the relations of the young Negro fell upon the host, and killed him, and the people said they had done well." Once the man knew that, even by accident, he had eaten his xina, he would notice something was wrong, and he would go to the Nganga of the fetish set apart for that particular crime, and get the thing righted, or suffer sickness or death, as the case might be. I grant Miss Kingsley that if a native gave another his xina to eat, and that person died within a decent period, he would feel he had murdered him ; so that when casca was given to him to eat as an ordeal, he would die in almost the exactly same way as that in which the young Negro in the story did. All of which proves the terrible hold fear mixed with imagination has over the Fjort's mind and stomach. A pot in which any xina has been cooked is unclean for ever, as far as that person is concerned, and no amount of washing will do. As I have said, xina are general and particular. The pig is xina to all royal blood; the Ampa kala, or buffalo, to the Bakutu, as a punishment to them for not listening to the words of Maloango; the antelope to a family round about Fahi, for refusing to give water to a voice in the bush when asked for it; fish of certain inland waters to certain people, near Cabinda, for not giving water to Nzambi and her child; and so on. The Fjort believes in the " voice that speaks," and this voice (as the very soul of man) is taken from the dead father and placed in the head of a living relation, and it speaks to the dead man's offspring, and thus what was his xina becomes the xina of his offspring. This is what the reverend fathers would call " conversing with the devil."

APPENDIX II.

FJORT SONGS.

THE following songs and additional matter by Mr. Dennett reached the Editor's hands in letters after the rest of the book was in type. As they contained valuable illustrations of the native customs and modes of thought, it was determined to add them by way of Appendix. Unfortunately the photographs of the string of symbols and the mode of using it were in such a condition that it was found impossible to reproduce them. Mr. Dennett's description, however, is so clear that their reproduction is hardly necessary.

The Editor has to thank Miss Kingsley for arranging the translation and explanation furnished by Mr. Dennett of the Song of Hunger, and for further elucidating some of its obscurities. His practice has been to give a translation of each word of the song separately, and at the end of a line or phrase to paraphrase the whole or translate it as closely as the differences of idiom of Bantu and Aryan languages permit. It was thought too tedious to reproduce this procedure in the case of every song; hence, in four out of the five songs here printed, only the translation or paraphrase of the entire line or phrase is given. In the case of the Song of Hunger, however, Mr. Dennett's procedure has been retained, as an illustration of the construction of the Bantu song.

The name given to the first of the following songs is Miss Kingsley's suggestion.

It should be noted that the symbol X stands throughout for *tch* or *dj*.

THE SONG OF LIFE.

I now have the pleasure of enclosing two photographs, representing, the one a string of symbols or headings of a native song, and the other the boy singing the song from the string.

The song itself and the string came from the Mayumba district, *i.e.*, that country to the north and east of Loango.

The string is composed of pieces of stick, shells, calabashes, and skins and feathers strung together.

1st line.	A piece of rounded stick about an inch long.
2nd ,,	The shell of a peanut.
3rd ,,	A piece of rounded stick with two notches in it.
4th ,,	Two pieces of rounded stick (two wives of the dead represented by a small bundle of cloth).
5th ,,	A piece of rounded stick (ximanga liambu).
6th ,,	Two pieces of rounded stick (ngoma and mavungu).

7th line   A piece of calabash (ntumbu).

8th „   Two pieces of rounded stick (two women).

One little piece of mandioca.

One piece of husk of palm-kernel.

9th „   One piece of rounded stick (one woman, Buketi).

10th „   „   „   with string round it (nganga nsassi).

11th „   „   „   (Buyali).

One piece of hollow wood for canoe.

12th „   One rounded piece of calabash (sun).

One half-moon-shaped piece of calabash (moon).

13th „   One short piece of round stick (two notches).

One small round stick (hammer).

One small bundle of cloth (Bisakala).

14th „   One piece of wood in shape of cross supposed to represent man
with drum between his legs.

A very small piece of wood as drumstick.

15th „   One round piece of wood (xivunda).

One smaller piece (son).

A bit of the leaf of Indian corn.

16th „   A flat piece of wood representing bark of a tree.

17th „   Round piece of stick with string round top (Nganga bi
yango).

18th „   Round piece of stick, one notch (son).

Small piece of stick, drumstick (ngoma).

19th „   Flat piece of stick like spoon (cease eating).

20th „   Two little bits of stem of tobacco (pipe and tobacco).

21st „   Small flat stick (xibala nganzi).

22nd „   Rather long round stick with forked stick tied round the
top representing Father Makuika, a prisoner.

23rd „   Small piece of pipe.

24th „   Round piece of stick tied round the middle.

25th „   Small piece of grass.

26th „   Shell.

27th „   Imitation of a comb.

Piece of wood like hand-mirror.

28th „   Round stick tied to string ¾ way up.

29th „   Skin of Mpakasa.

30th „   Tail of Ngumba.

Piece of skin.

31st „   Piece of skin of big antelope (sungu).

32nd „   Tail-feather of parrot (nkusu).

„   „   pheasant (mbulu nkoko).

So much, then, for the symbols; now for the song. One boy holds one end of the string while the singer holds the other; then, as the latter sings, his fingers touch the symbols. He sings a sentence, the other boy and the onlookers repeat it.

1. Xitini xinkondo xifumina ku Sundi. (Shoots of the silk-cotton tree came from Sundi.)*

2. Lunguba lu nkuanji lu fumina ku Sundi. (And peanuts, which are now so common also, came from Sundi.)†

3. Ma ngombi xinanga nquanga. (O, mother, ngombi dance the nquanga.)

4. Xibaïa niombo bakanga vulubongo. (Tie up the corpse in native grass-cloth.)

5. Ximanga liambu buna ku manga busu ku bititi. (The man who does not wish to hear the word turns his face to the grass.)

6. Ngoma i Mavungu ba nkote mi kunji. (Ngoma and Mavungu [Truth and Falsehood] are present at all palavers.)

7. Ntumpunganga ntumpu ilanga ma bungu. (Tell us openly the palaver you have hidden in your heart.)

8. Bilezi bixentu ku yolo, biyolo m'uenda ku lindaïa. (Two young ladies after smearing themselves over with takula, or red paint, go to visit their lovers.)

9. Buketi nkuendanga ku buala, keti nkuendanga ku buala kutanga babota. (Buketi keeps on going to town, going to town [because she is pregnant; may she] bring forth her child well.)

10. Nganga Nsassi Kubóla ku mbóla. (Nganga Nsassi [Suami] is sick.)

11. Buyali ku buyali tuala ko nlungu, mino ku simika nlungu muana ku banda. ([A man on the other side of the river shouts] "Buyali, Buyali, bring hither thy canoe [I want to cross this river]." [Buyali answers]: "I am pushing my canoe along with a bamboo; my child is at the bottom of the river.")

12. Ntangu mu luanda, ngondo ne bi sunji. (The sun is always marching [as in a hammock], and meets the new moon on the beach.)

13. Nkubi nyundu 'mduda bi sengo, kududa, kududa, mioko u aka nxienzo, bonga bi sakala u dudila bi sengo. (The blacksmith by beating makes the hoe; he beats and beats the iron until his hammer [too hot to

* And now fishermen in Cabinda, etc., make their nets and floats from its bark.

† Sundi is the grass country beyond the Mayomba district.

hold] drops to the ground. [Says his friend :] " Take this bit of native cloth to hold your hammer with, and go on beating the iron and make your hoe.")

14. Akubemba ndungu kubemba i xikonko. ([He addresses the drummer :] "Take your drum and put it between your legs, and your drum-stick, and beat the drum.")

15. Xivunda xibuala xinkenia li sango, kukenia kukenia li eno li aka nxienzo ; bikela muana mudidi ku manisia li sango. (When a man in town is old and eats Indian corn, he leaves some corn on the cob ; and the corn he leaves, his son is forced to finish.)

16. Lubalu lubaluka vi xifumba ? (How is it my family respect me no longer ?)

17. Nganga biyango biyango ba sumuka. (Some one has touched my birth-fetish [nganga biyango], and it has lost its virtue.)

18. Muana mbèla ngoma mi ntomba. (My child is sick ; fetch the ngoma [little drum.])

19. Bika i lia malandu e landu landu mabungu. (Let me eat malandu [a fruit] and remember the whole palaver.)*

20. Sungu mu xi timba, liamba mu nkondo. ([Put] tobacco in the pipe, liamba [hemp] in the calabash.)

21. Xibala nganzi balanga mabungu. (To think heavily, with a frown on one's forehead [nganzi], about the palaver).

22. Tata makuika bueka bonso mbi lilanga bueka ieka mu xivanga. (Father Makuika, who is a prisoner, is saluted by his sons, and answers : " Don't salute me ; can't you see the yoke on my neck ? ")

23. Nkonko xitumba bakulu bito babika. (An old pipe left by a relation must not be thrown away.)

24. Muamba sango ntiti bilongo. (Renowned muamba [yellow-tree] is our medicine-tree.)

25. Xizika zika nzila nkulu ntu bititi. (Xizika [grass with great roots] is the old man of the road [nkulu ntu = wischead.])

26. Seve nganga sevanga mabungu. (The laugher hears good words and goes on laughing.)

27. Kusimba xisanu ku simbuanga lu emuéno. (When you comb your hair, hold the glass before you.)

28. Xisinza mazila umananga milembo. (Stumps on the road keep on damaging one's toes.)

29. Mapakasa xinuaini ntuandi u tabuka. (The buffalo fights until his head falls off.)

---

* The malandu is a fruit given to a man to give him the power of remembering, and the will to speak all that is hidden in his heart.

30. Nzau e xilanga, ngumba imimbiekesi. (The elephant has a tail [the hairs of which are a valuable ornament], the porcupine has spines.)

31. Sungu kulila mu binanga. (Sungu [the name of a very large kind of antelope] eats on the top of hills.)

32. Nkusu mu nkunda, nbulu nkoko kuta nilolo. (The parrot perches on a branch, the pheasant sings his song [ko, ko, ko, ku, ku.])

SONG OF THE BURIAL OF THE FJORT PRINCE.

It has been a very difficult matter to get the song together. One cannot pick it up while they are singing it, for many of the words are new to one ; and to sit out of sight, perhaps in a cramped position, from 7 p.m. until 4 a.m. is no joke, and not an aid to one's work. To go openly to such a meeting means either a disturbance of the peace or a change in the programme. Then when one has got the rough part done and begins to ask questions about the song, the native "fights shy." He is sufficiently accustomed to the white man's ways to know that he will not give him credit for being serious, and he does not like his ways laughed at It needs a native (if he is a good man) of great moral courage to tell a white man these things ; and if he is a bad one he must be a great villain, without any sense of respect for the white man he is conversing with, to speak upon such a subject. It is greatly to the Fjort's credit that he is not worse and more degraded than he is, for he has forgotten the deep meaning of the words he uses, which perhaps would keep him pure in thought in the midst of his "worship" (?) of maternity, or earth as the mother and bearer of all things. Watching the Fjort at his burial ceremonies, and not knowing the meaning of the words of his song, no one could possibly detect the slightest sign of indecency. Some who, as Chicaia said, had shame, wore the leaves of the mandioca before their persons, and these were under the influence of

Christianity. Personally, the pure and unadulterated heathen seemed to me the more decent of the two, naked as he was, for he, like the half-naked stoker on board a steamer, struck me as a *man* who had a certain work to do, and was not afraid to do it.   *   *   *   *

The Fjort either destroys the house in which his late relative dwelt after burial, or else dismantles it and sells the material to some other family. He plants mandioca in the ground where the deceased's bed rested, so that people shall not build there again. The wives sleep in the shimbec with the corpse, but none of the family dare sleep in it after the burial of the deceased, for fear of being considered his poisoner or be-witcher. They fear a meeting with the ghost, or chimbindi, of the deceased, for no one has been known to live more than two days after having been beaten by one.

I took instantaneous photographs of the shimbec and coffin of my cook's father, whose death and burial I have related.

In my walks through KaCongo it was by no means a rare occurrence to come across a place where orange, lime, and mango-trees were found growing in a half-wild state; levelled terraces, raised foundations, and neglected mandioca planta-tions clearly pointed to the fact that a village had once existed there. Upon enquiry I found that these places had been deserted, owing to the number of deaths from small-pox. This is one of the reasons why a prince, although he may have a fine house, generally lives in a small shimbec by the side of it. This custom may also be one of the reasons why the Fjort is, as a rule, so poorly housed, apart from the fear he has of being considered a witch if he builds himself a substantial dwelling.

If millionaires at home were as easily frightened by the Socialists, where should we all be?

Now for the song. It is past sundown, and the relations and friends about to bury their chief are seated around the coffin, that as yet does not contain the corpse. That relation who has undertaken the burial now arises, and beating the coffin with his hand, cries out:

1. "Mpolo ku fu." (Bene est mori et quiescere.)

Again he hits the coffin, and cries:

2. "Mpola makata." (Testiculi bene quiescunt.)

Again he beats the case, and shouts:

3. "Mpolo xikolo." (Cunnus bene quiescit.)
4. "Mpolo msutu." (Penis bene quiescit.)
5. "Ku fua nkulu u tuba bu ao." (Et spiritus mortuus est et dicendi facultas.)

Then the people there assembled take off their clothes, and, after the chief mourner has sung the following verse, burst forth in song, repeating the same words and tune time after time.

1. "Ku aba si tuli monanga." (In olden days of the earth [these good things] were often seen.)

The song is now changed to:

2. "Basi uanda liboili banonga mpakala bikolo." (Basi [the Basi, or secret society] illius oppidi saccum virginitatum habent.)

This song is sung by all until they are tired of it, when another one is given out, and so on.

3. "Bakakata boili umquenda o." (The old folk of the town are all dying.)

4. Aujéi ko u rata mikala abu uaka mkuta 'mpinda" (You did not plant nor hoe, and now you have a basket of peanuts ; [where did you get it ?].)

5. " Néno uak'ili bulu msutu nako uvanga li bulu." (Vulva cavea est, quam fecit penis.)

6. " Beno ni kufulanga nkossa ubilo nkéia kubenga nkossa kubengila nyamu milénji." (You are always asking about the lobster ; don't you know that its teeth [mouth] are misplaced, and that when you boil it, it becomes red up to its hair ?)

7. " Xilumbu xina xinquenda yaia masuella kwitekanga." (The day that my brother goes [dies] I keep on shedding tears.)

8. " Ma mbamba* songa nèno uvisia munu uaka enxienzo." (Mambamba, utere cunno bene, donec os ejus doleat.)

9. " Abu lélé makata mavia mbazu." (Dum dormis, testiculi ardent).

10. " Abu lélé msutu mavia mbazu." (Dum dormis, ardet penis.)

11. " Abu lélé xikoalo xavia mbazu." (Dum dormis, ardet cunnus.)

Then comes the final part of this song :

12. " Una uku vena uli ku linda mayaka ma mona u lili obua." (One gives without being asked.   The new mandioca one plants, another eats.)

Then the people sing ordinary songs until the cock crows ; then they put the corpse into the coffin.   The wife of the dead prince then places a small gourd into a " matet," or basket, and goes to the place she has been in the habit of going to fetch water.   On arriving there, she falls into the water once, twice, three times, and her part in the ceremony of the burial of the Fjort is at an end, and she is free.

When the wife has left the coffin, the chief mourner again sings :

13. " Mingenza monami kuluma tuenda Kamango † u fua." (Young man, my son, push and go ; Kamango is dead.)

14. " Mueniyambi ‡ ngulubu xina xikoada ku lia." (Mueniyambi, they

---

* Ma mbamba is said by the Fjort to be the name of a man of old, and to-day he attaches no meaning to the name.

† Kamango, they say, is the name of an old prince.

‡ Mueniyambi, another prince of old.

said, did not eat pig [but one day he asked them what it was he was eating, and they had to admit that] he was eating the foot of a pig.)

Then the coffin is placed in the hole dug for it, and the earth is heaped up over it by willing hands; and as the Fjort throws the earth upon the coffin, he murmurs:

"Bakulu * vandu vandu." (People of spirit-land, be at rest, be at rest [and don't bother the people of this world].)

THE SONG OF THE SNAKE.

1. Sanguila mboma kumina muntu.
2. Mbelli sandangu nkambu ku vonda muntu.
3. Aula mani Zinga bazolila muliambu.
4. Bakana † ku vonda, ba vonda kua u—
5. Macosso muana Danka banzola maka lilanga.

1. [Si quis, in oppidum cum venerit, dicat] anguem parvulum hominem devorasse, [nemo ei credat. Sic Fjort cum primum de pæderastia audivisset, non verum esse credidit.]

2. [Ut inter saltantes opus est] cuivis cultro, quo nescio quem [illudentem] occidat: [sic Fjort, cum primum audivisset aliquem hoc facinus, in se admisisse, cultrum desideravit, quo eum occidere].

3. Filius Zingæ, [cujus facies velut] gum-copal [pulchra erat], pœderastiæ deditus erat.

---

* Bakulu—*Nkulu*, as I have already described to you, is that part of the dead which the Fjort says can be placed in the head of a living person; *Ba*, Bantu people; *Kulu*, perhaps soul, spirit. The Fjort say that the Bakulu are invisible and that they cannot see one another; but they contradict themselves, for on referring to my notes I find that when a man wishes to become rich, he obtains a fetish, or nkissi, called Buti, and when a man who has obtained this fetish dies, his nkulu ties up other Bakulu, and places them in the corner of some shimbee, and keeps them there.

† Zinga means *the long-lived*; Bakana, *the calculator, the man of thought.*

4. Bakana [eum] occidere [voluit, et filius Zingæ respondit:] Occide [me, si vis, at ego in flagitio pergam].

5. Macosso, puer Dankæ [albi hominis] dominum amabat, [et quum hic in Europam abiisset] non desiit lugere].

THE SONG OF LOANGO WOMEN.

1. Munu u li vumba lelo u xinda ku vata mama.

2. Muango ma woho ba li aku bunkuela anjéa ku kuela mpé.

3. Ku simba va nxenzo, ku simba va ku bella, malongo, malongo mabila nkumbu.

4. Minu uali aku mama.

5. Ndumba buala lelo uiza muinhi.

6. Suaka esesi lelo xinda ku sala.

7. Minu uali aku mama

8. Zimvula ziamana.

1. Tu mater cui os est magnum, multum serere debes.

2. Tu qui permultum saltas [nuptæ mulieres dicunt] desine saltare, et nube tu quoque.

3. Mulier salax, quæ huc illuc (multa loca) visitat, sed si quando cum ea vis coire, morbum nescio quem semper pro excusatione habet.

4. Forsitan quæ propria sint tibi palam faciam, O mater.

5. Meretrix in urbem interdiu venire solet [dum nuptæ mulieres in villa restant].

6. Gracilis mulier opus suum bene perficit.

7. Forsitan [etc., ut supra (4)].

8. Imbres cessant [id est, hoc carmen de mulieribus, quæ per imbres serunt, finitum est].

THE SONG OF HUNGER.

1. Xissanga e Buali bi koka mti
2. Muanyali ba nlambili xikamvu
3. Xinkatu nkatu manyonga
4. Lembe li Ngongo ngeia tubanga
5. Tubanga minu i lembo
6. Xilunga e Quillo bi koka mti
7. Xilunga uaka xi nanu
8. Nzala nguli yalla tanta
9. Ndevo nkunda mbongo
10. Bemvena madungo masina mbinda
11. Zimvula zi Maloango ziaku zimani
12. Xilumbu mfuafua minu kuxibota.

1. *Xissanga*, a province of Loango ; *e*, and ; *Buali*, another province of Loango ; *bi*, they ; *koka*, drag ; *mti*, a tree.

    Explanation.—In these provinces the people are dying of hunger, and are therefore making new farms in the Fjort way, clearing forest and dragging about the trees as a sort of rough ploughing.

2 & 3. *Muanyali*, proper name meaning the first stage of pregnancy; *ba nlambili*, cooked; *xikamvu*, large basket used for carrying food ; *Xinkatu*, mat on which food is served ; *nkatu*, mat; *manyonga*, to feel bitterly in one's heart.

    Muanyali gets a large basket and a mat of the right kind, and cooked food, and is angry that the basket and the mat are all right, the food is properly cooked, but there is not enough. This is a common African way of indirectly saying disagreeable things or telling you what they dislike in a thing. "This is right," they say, "and

M

that is right;" and they expect you to know what is
wanting.   It is as if they set you a subtraction sum:
given the total, you deduct what is praised, and the
difference is what is disliked. If you don't arrive at it,
you are a fool, and it is no use talking to you.

4 & 5. *Lembe* (the name given to a wife married according
to the rites of Lemba, *i.e.*, the wife, properly so called, who
binds herself not to survive her husband), the wife of Muanyali;
li ngongo (a large fish-eating bird—a pelican), proper name;
ngeia, thou; *tubanga*, talk; *minu*, I; *lembo*, cease.

Muanyali's wife, Lembe, asks her father, Mr. Pelican,
to explain to her husband why she has not been able to
send him more food. She says to her father: "You talk
to him about it; I cease from telling him." That is, it is
no good my telling him, he thinks I could send more if
I chose.   Then off goes Pelican to his son-in-law, and
says:

6 & 7. *Xilunga e Quillo li koku mti*, Xilunga and Quillo
are dying of hunger (details explained above); *Xilunga*, a
province of Loango; *uaka*, now; *xi nanu*, is far away.

I think this means: " We who live in Quillo (a province
of Loango) can get nothing, even if we go to Xilunga,
because that is famine-stricken too." I know, *xi nanu*,
far away, is often used as a description of a place not worth
going to.

8. *Nzala*, through; *nguli*, mother; *yalla*, hunger; *tanta*,
pain.

" The thought of the hungered mother pains them." Pelican throws this observation in, meaning Xilunga and Quillo grieve for their hungering mothers.

9. *Ndevo,* beard; *nkunda,* elephant's tail; *mbongo,* money.

I think Pelican throws out a suggestion that a man named Ndevo nkunda is a rich man, and should be asked for aid; "money," of course, not being necessarily coin, but possibly in this case food.

10. *Bemrena,* efficiunt; *madungo,* testiculos tumefactos; *masina,* fundum; *mbinda,* cucurbitæ.

Mulieres viros ita elephantiasi afficiunt, ut testiculi ventri cucurbitæ similes fiunt. (A statement not made in the interest of medical knowledge, but connected in the African mind with the rainfall, and having a definite bearing on what falls.) Pelican is still speaking.

11. *Zimvula,* rain; *zi Maloango,* as in the days of Maloango; *ziaku,* they; *zimani,* are finished.

"Now we no longer get the rains we had in the days of Maloango."

12. *Xilumbu,* day; *mafuafua,* die; *minu,* I; *kuxi bota,* to be well.

"I shall be well cared for the day I die;" I shall be well buried. That is, I wish I were dead. This is the final lament of poor Pelican.

INDEX.

Adultery, see Crimes, Sexual Relations
Agriculture, xx., 18, 19, 161
Ajumba tribe, x.
Alfonso I., King of Congo, xxii.
Ambassador, Story of Nzambi Mpungu's, 105
Amulets, 136, see Charms, Spells
Angola, xvii., xxi.
—— Expulsion of priests from, xx.
Angoy, Kingdom of, xv., xxiv., 2
—— successor to the throne of, always put to death the next day, xxxii.
Animals, Helpful, 7, 36, 74, 103, 126
Animals, lower, spoken of as human beings, 3, 10, 11
—— stories of, 35, 69, 71, 74, 77, 82, 85, 90, 94, 98, 106, 123, 124
Antelope and the Leopard, story of the, 71
—— story of the Rabbit and the, 90
—— in other stories, 77, 82, 123, 125
Anyambie, god of the Mpongwe, 119

Bafan, The, vii.
Balloon, story of Ngomba's, 49
Bantu, religion, xiii.
—— tribes, xxxi.
Barbot, vi.
—— quoted, xiv.
Bastian, Dr., iii.
Battel, Andrew, cited, xvii.
Bavili, tribe of Fjorts, xix., xxxi.
Benin, Bight of, vii., xiii.
Benito, River, vii.
Bimbindi, spirits of the dead, 11, 115, 156
—— stories of, 11, 12, 14, 15, 16

Bingo, rites of, 4
Bird-messengers, story of the, 103
Birth customs and superstitions, 19, 137
Black, Why some men are white, others black, 18, 101
Boma, 5, 11
Bombangoij, city, xv.
Boomba, form of marriage, 72
Bosi, see Mbosi
Bosman, vi.
Bride-wagers, 35, 74
—— incident of the Supplanted, 128
Brother who knew more than the elder, story of the younger, 65
Brothers, story of the Twin, ii., 60
—— story of the three, 108
Brue, Sieur, vi.
Buchholz, iii.
Burial customs and superstitions, 22, 23, 55, 110, 155
—— places, 5
—— song, 155
Burton, Sir R. F., ix.

Cabinda, port in Angoy, xvi., xx., xxiv., 5, 94
Calabar, people, xxvi.
Cameroons, xiii.
Cannibalism, xiv.
Caõ, Diego, discoverer of the Congo, xvii.
Capuchin Fathers, adventures of two, xiv., xvi.
—— Missionaries, allies of the Portuguese, xvi., xxiii., xxiv.
Casca, use of, 17, 23, 48, 92, 140, 145
Cat and the Gazelle, story of the Wild, 85

Charms, use of, 4, 6, 9, 10, 17, 20, 60, 115
Chegilla, see Kazila
Child, story of how Kengi lost her, 58
—— story of the wonderful, ix., 56
Chimbindi, see Bimbindi
Chimpanzee and Gorilla, story of the, 69
Chimpanzu, river and spirit, 5
Christian influence in native religion, xxi., 120
Circumcision, 4, 20
Clouds, beliefs as to, 7
Coffin, see Burial
Congo Belge, xxi.
—— Français, viii.
Congo, Kingdom of, xiii., xiv., xvii., xviii., xxiii.
—— extent of, in 1875, xxi.
—— kings of, xxi., xxii., and see Fumu Congo
—— natives of, xxv.
—— River, vii., xiv., xviii., xx., 1, 4, 118
—— discovery of xvii., xviii.
—— Islands in, 5
Coronation of prince, xxxii., 4
Creation, no legends of the, 18
—— stories of the, 120, 124, 127
Creator, see Nzambi Mpungu
Crimes, criminal procedure and punishments, xi., xix., xxviii., 16, 21, and see Justice
—— in tales, 48, 54
Crocodile does not eat the Hen, story of why the, ix., 106 ; cited in pleading, xi., xii.
—— story of the Leopard and the, 98
Crocodiles and witchcraft, xxix, 5
Culture-legends, 18, 118

Dead, festivals in honour of the, 24
Death-customs, see Burial
Debt, almost universal, 22
Deities, West African, xix., and see Anyambie, Earth, Fetish, Images, Mbuiri, Mongo, Nkissi nsi, Nzambi, Nzambi Mpungu, Rain-giving god, Sunga
—— Travelling, disguised, 121, 122
Dennett, R. E., i., viii., ix., xviii., xix., xxiv.

Dennett, R. E., Notes by, on Introduction, xxxi.
—— Notes by, on Appendix I., 146
—— Opinions of, on Nkissism, discussed, xii., xiv., 118, 147
—— Statements by, on Kazila, discussed, xxvii., xxviii.
Descent into Hell, ii., and see Brothers, The Twin
Difficulties of collecting and interpreting West African folklore, ii., 119
Divination, 16, 111, 140
Dondo in Angola, xvii.
Dreams, influence of, 17, 141
Drowning, rescue from, 8
Dutch break up Portuguese power in Congo, xxiii.

Earth, Mother, 4, 118, 119, 131, 132
—— Spirit, 5, 118
Eggs, not eaten, xxix.
Ellis, Col. A. B., ix.
Ewè-speaking peoples, ix., x.
Exorcism, 17

Fan tribes, x.
February sacred to Nkissi nsi, 136
Festivals, 24, 137
Fetish, in tales, 43, 60, 88, 94, 96
—— of Chilunga, story of the, 96
—— religion, xiii., xiv., xviii., xxi., 134
—— rites and belief, 2, 3, 9, 11, 96, 112, 113, 115, 135, 136, 146, 159
—— Sunga punished my greatuncle's twin brother Basa, story of How the, 88
Fetishes, story of the Fight between the Two, 94
Fire, descent of, ii., 7, 74
—— legend of the first use of, 18
Fish and fishermen, 8, 19, 25, 49, 88
Fjort agriculture, 19, 161
—— beliefs, 10, 18
—— language, 118, 119
—— religion, xviii., xx., xxi., xxii., xxx., 1, 117
—— songs, 150
—— tribes, xviii., xix., xxxi., 1, 119
Flemish missionaries, xiii.
Fool, story of the Smart Man and the, 25
Forests, superstitions as to, 9
Franciscans, xvi., xxiii.
French rule, xxi.

Friends who quarrelled, story of the
　Two, 31
Fumu Kongo, King of Congo, xii.,
　xiv., xvi., xvii., xix., xx., xxi.,
　xxxi., 1, 2, 10, 134
Fumu, meaning of, xxxi., 1
Funeral, see Burial
Funzi, form of marriage, 20, 72
──── the Blacksmith, 7, 18

Gaboon people, xxvi.
Gagas, cannibal tribe, xvii., xxii.
Gangas, see Ngangas
Gazelle and the Leopard, story of the,
　82
──── got married, story of How the,
　35
──── story of the Wild Cat and the,
　85
Gindes, see Gagas
Gold Coast, xxi.
Goldie, Rev. H., v.
Gorilla, native name for, 3
──── story of the Chimpanzee and,
　69
Gum-copal, 19, 139, 159

Heaven, journey to, 74, 133
Hell, descent into, ii., and see Brothers
Hen, see Crocodile
Hospitality, want of, punished, 121,
　122
Hunger, song of, 150, 161
Hunters and hunting, 18, 19
Husband, story of the Wicked, 54, and
　see Wife

Ibet, see Kazila
Images, 2, 4, 9, 112, 113, 135, 136, 138,
　146
Imbuiri, see Ombuiri
Industries, see Agriculture, Fish, Hun-
　ters, Iron, Manufactures, Pottery
Iron and other smiths' work, xx., 18,
　19
Italian missionaries, xiii.
Ivili, see Bavili
Ivory coast, xxi.

Jesuits, xx., xxiii.
Joaõ II., King of Portugal, xxii.
Johnston, Sir H. H., xiii.
Justice, administration of native, xi.,
　141, and see Crimes ; in tales, 48, 55,
　59, 126, 141, 144

Kabinda, see Cabinda
Ka-Congo, family of, 108
──── King of, xv., xvi., xvii., 2,
　21, 22, and see Fumu Kongo
──── province and people of, viii.,
　xii., xiii., xiv., xvii., xviii.,
　xix., xx., xxi., xxiii., 1, 7, 94, 114,
　139
Karkola River, iii.
Kazila, explained, xxvi., 137, 147
──── instances of, xxix., 10, 122, 148
──── Merolla's account of, xxv.,
　xxviii.
Kengi lost her child, story of How, 58
King of Congo, xxi., and see Fumu
　Kongo, Alfonso I.
Kingsley, Miss, adventure on the Kar-
　kola River, iii.
Kinsembo, 1
Kongo, see Congo

Lake formed to punish want of hospi-
　tality, 121, 122
Languages, necessity of studying Afri-
　can, v.
Law, Doctrine of Native, that igno-
　rance is not to be punished unless
　culpable ignorance, xxviii.
──── Examples of Native : how an
　injured man obtains help against
　his enemies, iii. ; in tales, 48, 55,
　59, and see Crimes, Justice
Lemba, or Lembe, form of marriage,
　20, 72, 162
Leopard and the Crocodile, story of
　the, 98
──── killing a, 80
──── punished the turtle, How the,
　77
──── story of the Antelope and
　the, 71
──── story of the Gazelle and the,
　82
──── the royal animal, beliefs and
　practices as to the, 9, 80
Life, restoration to, folktale incident,
　33, 64
──── song of, 151
──── story of How the wives restored
　their husband to, 33
Lightning, superstition as to, 7, and
　see Funzi
Lion in love, folktale incident of the,
　71
Literature, branches of native oral, ix.
Loanda, xx.

Loango, province and kingdom of, xii., xiii., xiv., xvi., xvii., xviii., xix., xx., xxi., xxiii., 1, 2, 11, 22, 114, 162
―――― population, xxxi.
―――― women, song of, 160
Loango Luz, River, 21
Locusts, 11
Loge, River, 1
Lulondo, River and spirit, 6

Mafumu, title of under-kings of provinces, xxxi., 2
Makongo, king of Congo, xvii., xxxii.
Malandu, fruit, use of, 154
Maloango, 21, 163
Man, story of the turtle and the, 77
Manifumu, see Mafumu
Manufactures, xx., 19
Marriage customs and superstitions, 20, 72
―――― forms of, 20 72
Mayumba district, 151
Mbosi, Lake, 10, 122
Mbuiri, god or spirit of the Mpongwe, 119
Mbunzi, the south-west wind, 10, 11
Medicine and medical practice, 4, 9
Medicines, see Amulets, Charms, Spells
Medusa-witch, folktale incident of the, 60
Men, difference in colour of, how caused, 18, 101
Merolla, quoted, xv., xxiii., xxv.
―――― statement of, on Chegilla, discussed, xxviii., 147
Mfuzi, the blacksmith, 7, 18
Milk of animals, not drunk, xxix.
Missionaries as authorities on African folklore, iii., v.
―――― influence of, on native religion, xxi., 119
―――― reports of, xiii., and see Roman Catholic
Mlomvu, River and spirit, 6
Mohammedan influences in native religion, xxi.
Mongo, mountain, xix.
―――― legends of, 5
Monkey Island, 5
Monteiro, J. J., quoted, xx.
Month, division of the, 8
Moon, legend of the, 6
―――― new, ceremony, 7
Mpongwe-speaking tribes, xix., 135
―――― gods of, 119

Mpungu, meaning of, 3
Mungo, see Mongo
Musurongo, xxxii., 137
―――― Nkissi of the, 138

Names, of natives after animals, 9
―――― secret, 35
Nassau, Rev. Dr., v., x., xxix.
Nature-spirits, see Deities
Ncanlam, chief of the Musurongo, xxxii.
Ndotchi, poisoner and witch, 16, 112, 114, 131, and see Witch, Witchcraft
Negro religion, xiii., xiv., xxv., xxvi.
Ngangas, xii., xiv., xviii., xx., 2, 9, 12, 16, 17, 23, 111, 112, 135, 136, 138, 139, 140, 146
―――― classes of, 2, 4
Ngoio, a rain-doctor, xxxii., 2
―――― native embassies to, 2, 11
Ngomba's balloon, story of, 49
Ngunie River, xix.
Niari River, xxii.
Niger Coast Protectorate, vii.
―――― Company, Royal, vii.
―――― River, vii., xxi.
Nkissi and Nkissism, xii., xiii., xiv., xviii., xx., 1, 2, 4, 9, 18, 112, 115, 117, 119, 131, 134, 136, 137, 138, 146
Nkissi nsi, spirit of the earth, 1, 2, 3, 133, 135, 136
Ntandu dialect, 3
Nzambi, ii., 117
―――― cult of, 3
―――― drum of, story of the, 123, 124
―――― footsteps of, 130
―――― in stories, 2, 7, 18, 60, 74, 106, 120, 121, 122, 123, 128
―――― introduction of the cult of, xii, 133
―――― meaning of name, 2, 118, 131.
―――― stories of, their value, ix.
Nzambi Mpungu, the Creator, 2, 3, 18, 120, 124, 131, 132, 133
―――― causes tides, 9
―――― his fire stolen, 7
―――― in stories, 74, 103, 105
Nzambi Mpungu's ambassador, story of, 105
Nzambi's daughter, story of How the spider won and lost, 74
―――― marriage of, 60, 128

Offerings, see Sacrifices
Ogowé, River and district, xiii., xix.
Ogre, in tales. 50, and see Bimbindi
Oil rivers, xiii.
Okanda River, xix.
Ombuiri, supernatural being of Mpongwe tribes, xix., xx., 119
Omens, 8
Ordeals, 17, 23, 48, 92, 112, 114, 139, 140, 145
Oroungou country, iii.
Orunda, see Kazila
Otherworld, journey to, 133, and see Heaven, Hell

Paint-house, 4, 20, 22, 50
Palavers, see Justice
Partnership, the story of a, 143
Pelican, 162
Philtres, 17
Pillars of clay, human beings transformed into, 5
Pleading, see Justice
Poisoning, crime of, xxviii., 16, 17, and see Ndotchi
Polygamy, see Marriage
Ponta da Lenha, 4
Pottery, 19
Protuguese, discovery of Congo by the, xiii., xvii.
———— missionaries, xiii., xvii
———— navagators, early, xiii.
———— political power and influence of the, xvi., xvii., xx., xxi. xxii., xxiii., xxx.
Priesthood, 135, and see Ngangas
Prohibitions, see Kazila; in tales, 40, 43, 62
Prometheus, see Fire
Proverbs, Native African, examples of, 27, 142
———— importance of, ix.
Proyart, Abbé, quoted, xvi.
Puberty, rites of, 4, 20, 22, 128
Purification, rites of, 137, 158

Quillo, province of, 162
———— River, 1

Rabbit and the Antelope, story of the, 90
Rainbow, superstition as to, 6
Rainfall, belief as to, 163
Rain-doctor, xxxii., 2
Rain-giving god and his rites, 138, 139

Religion, xii., and see Bantu, Deities, Fetish, Images, Ngangas, Negro, Nkissism
Resurrection, see Life
Riddles, native African, ix.
Rivers, spirits of, 5, 88, 109, 118, 119
Rocks, superstitions as to, 4
Roman Catholic missionaries, xiii., xxiii.
———————————— Influence of, on the Fjort religion, xxii., xxx.

Sacrifices, 3, 8, 9, 96
St James, miracle of, xxiii.
San Salvador, throne-town of Congo, xviii., xx., xxi., 1, 2
Schlieden, Hubbe, iii.
Sea and lakes, towns under the, 9, 89
———————————— superstitions as to the, 8
———————————— symbolized by a crab, 9
Sexual relations, 20, 21, 145
Shekiani tribe, x.
Sierra Leone, xvii., xxi.
Sister, folktale incident of the Despised, 49
Sky, beliefs about the, 7
Slavery and slaves, xxvi., 8, 22
Smart Man and the Fool, story of the, 25
Snake, song of the, 159
Sogno, Count of, xiv., 138
———— province of, xvi.
Song of Burial of Fjort prince, 155
———— of Hunger, 150, 161
———— of Life, 151
———— of Loango Women, 160
———— of the Snake, 159
Songs, native African, difficulty of interpreting, ix.
———— Fjort, 150
———— how sung, 153
Souls, Catching, xxix.
———— doctrine of, 116
———— transferring soul of deceased, 115, 159
Spells, 17, 18, and see Amulets Charms
Spider won and lost Nzambi' Daughter, story of How the, ii., 7 74
Stanley Pool, i.
Stars, 7

Stories, classes of, ix.
—— historical, rare, ix.
—— how told, 25
—— legal, their use and value, x.
—— play-stories, xii.
—— position of, in native culture, ix.
Sun, legend of the, 6
Sunga punished my great-uncle's twin-brother, Basa, story of How the fetish, 6, 88
Sunken towns, see Hospitality, Lake
Symbols of native song, string of, 150, 151
—————————— how used, 153

Taboo, see Kazila, Prohibitions
Tar-baby, folktale incident of the, 92
Tekklifumu, title of subordinate chief, xxxi., xxxii.
Thunder, superstitions as to, 7
Totems, animal, unknown, xxvii.
Traders as authorities on African folk-lore, iii., vi.
—— lend money to native princes and traders, 22
Transformation, belief in the power of, 10
—————————— in tales, 5, 42, 52, 57. 105
Travellers often untrustworthy on African folklore, iii.
Tshi-speaking peoples, ix., x.
Turtle and the man, story of the, 77
Twin brother, Basa, story of How the fetish, Sunga, punished my great uncle's, 6, 88
—— brothers, story of the, 60
Twins, superstitious as to, 8

Unclean, means prohibited in Mr. Dennett's phraseology, xxix.

Vanishing wife, story of the, see Wife

Waddell, Rev. H. M., v.
Waterspouts, 8
Week, days of the, 8, 137
White, others black, story of Why some men are, 18, 101
Whitford, J., vi
Wife, folktale incident of the Super-natural, 39, 42
—— stealing, iv.
—— story of the ill-used, saved by her son, 28
—— story of the jealous, 46
—— story of the vanishing, i., 39, 42
Wilson, Rev. J. L., v., xxx.
Witchcraft, xxiii., 112, 114
Witch-doctors, 16
Witches dwell in forests, 9
—— fear of being considered, 150
—— treatment of dead, 6, 112, and see Ndotchi
Wives restored their husband to life, story of How the, 33
Wizards, xiv., and see Ndotchi, Witch-craft, Witches
Woman overreaches herself, story of the, 86
Woodpecker, see Animals, Helpful

Xina, see Kazila

Year, division of the, 8
Yoruba-speaking peoples, ix.

Zaire, see Congo river
Zimini, supernatural being under the sea, 9
Zinganga, see Ngangas

PRINTED BY J. B. NICHOLS AND SONS, PARLIAMENT MANSIONS, VICTORIA STREET, S.W.